Creative WINDOW *Treatments*

First published in the United Kingdom in 1998 by Hamlyn
an imprint of Reed Books Ltd.
Michelin House, 81 Fulham Road, London, SW3 6RB
and Auckland, Melbourne, Singapore and Toronto

ISBN 0 600 59440 8

Cover design by Senate

Cover photographs:
Front Cover Eaglemoss Publications Ltd./Steve Tanner (L);
Mark Wood (CB); Elizabeth Whiting & Associates (T; B; R);
Ikea Ltd. (C); *Front Flap* Reed International Books Ltd./Debi
Treloar; *Back Cover* Elizabeth Whiting & Associates (TR; R);
Reed International Books Ltd./Debi Treloar (TL); Di Lewis (L)

Printed and bound in Hong Kong

HAMLYN

Guide to Creating Your Home

Creative
WINDOW
Treatments

HAMLYN

Contents

The basics

Tips on choosing, making and hemming curtains

Start sewing

Complete instructions for over a dozen do-it-yourself curtain styles from effortless to more intricate

FINISHING TOUCHES

Make your own creative curtain accessories

BLINDS

Create your own or personalise bought blinds with paint and trimwork

CHOOSING CURTAINS

Take time to choose the best curtain treatment for your home – the right choice will not only enhance the windows but turn an ordinary room into a really special place.

When it comes to choosing curtains, there's no end to the different treatments and finishing touches on offer, in an exciting range of styles and fabrics. With so many options available, the key to success is to approach the task methodically. Consider the style, size and shape of the window, and what you want the curtains for. Are they simply decorative, or must they also keep out draughts? Should they be pulled back off the windows to let in light and frame a view, or is the scene outside better hidden? If privacy and insulation aren't important, perhaps you can dress your windows by draping fabric over a pole – a simple and effective treatment if you don't need to draw the curtains.

Think about the room too – its proportions and what it is used for, and the other soft furnishings. Do you want the curtains to be a focal point, or convey an understated elegance? Though lined curtains drape well and provide better insulation than unlined, easily laundered unlined curtains may be more practical in a playroom or kitchen.

Once you have sorted out your initial thoughts, work through the checklist overleaf to help you choose a curtain style that suits your needs.

Full-length curtains with a box-pleated valance are a fair match for a large sash window. Using tiebacks to hitch the sheers up with the curtains softens the imposing effect to suit the bedroom.

STYLE CHECKLIST

When choosing curtains it's a good idea to clarify your thoughts by separating off some of the different elements involved. Below is a quick checklist of questions to ask yourself. Look through them, then read on for possible solutions and a fuller description of any particular effects you want to create.

- ❖ What length?
- ❖ Hung from a pole or a track?
- ❖ Which heading?
- ❖ With or without a valance, pelmet or swags and tails?
- ❖ Hung straight or held with tiebacks?
- ❖ Lined or unlined?
- ❖ Combined with sheers or a blind?

WHAT LENGTH?

Sill-length curtains work well in cottage style rooms with recessed windows, or with horizontal windows in modern homes. Curtains should barely touch the sill.

Below-sill length can look untidy when drawn back – use a tieback or curtain holdback to drape them attractively. If you have a radiator under the window the curtains should be finished just above it.

Floor-length curtains work best at sash windows, in bays and bows and on French or picture windows. The curtains should almost touch the floor with no visible gap. Where the curtains won't get underfoot, you can let the fabric tumble, or puddle, on to the floor in arranged folds.

Café curtains give privacy at the lower half of the window while letting in light at the top.

▲ *Cornice rod and casing*
Lack of privacy is not a problem in this dining room, so the curtains, made with a casing slipped on to a cornice rod, remain drawn. The exposed rod is hidden by a shirred pole cover. The sheers on a separate track behind can be drawn.

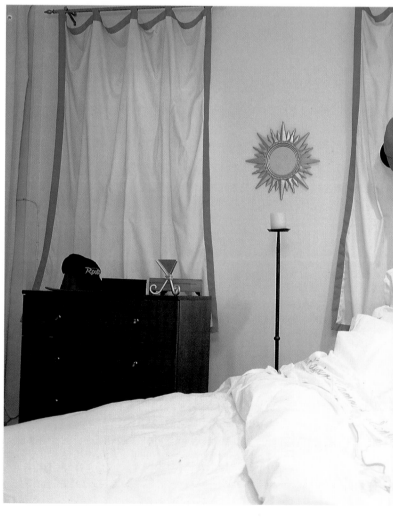

◀ **To sill height**
In a child's bedroom, using a curtain pole and snazzy fabrics for the sill-length curtains and blind hits just the right note of fun.

▶ **A goblet heading**
Hung on a bowed track with a formal, goblet pleated heading, these elegant curtains set the tone of the whole room. They are fixed at the centre and held back permanently by high, tasselled tiebacks to emphasize the height of the window.

◀ **A tab heading**
These inspiringly simple curtains are suspended from two delicate brass poles by means of loops, or tabs, of the red border fabric.

POLE OR TRACK?

Poles are a decorative and versatile option for hanging curtains. Points to consider include:
❖ Poles with a brass or metal finish for a formal look.
❖ Wood or plastic poles for an informal style.
❖ Slim, discreet poles for short informal curtains.
❖ Large poles for long straight runs, and to carry the weight of heavy floor-length curtains.

Curtains can be hung from poles in a number of ways. The fullness of the curtain can be taken up with a heading tape, then hung from rings. The curtain can be made with a tab heading (loops of fabric that go over the pole) or it can have a casing (a horizontal pocket that slides over the pole) and cannot be drawn. For dramatic effects with a pole, try draping swags or hanging a valance.

Tracks have a streamlined effect that suits many modern furnishing styles. Though most are functional rather than stylish, some decorative types are available. The curtains are hooked on to runners designed to glide smoothly along the track. Special points to look out for include:
❖Special lightweight plastic and aluminium tracks can be bent to fit bow and bay windows.
❖Steel tracks are available for the heaviest of curtains.
❖Combination tracks make hanging two curtains, or a curtain plus valance, extremely easy.

The fullness of the curtain can be gathered up in a range of heading styles which play an important role in the final look of the window dressing. The curtain heading usually covers the track; if there is no pelmet or valance, the curtain is best left undrawn, and held off the window with tiebacks so that it always conceals the plain track.

WHICH HEADING?

Headings determine the way that the fullness of the curtain or valance is gathered up. They range from simple gathered headings through to elaborate smocked and pleated types. The most commonly used headings are gathers, and pencil, triple, cylindrical and cartridge pleats.

Casings are the simplest way to hang a curtain. A hem is stitched along the top of the curtain, then it is gathered on to the pole. The width of the hem can vary from a meagre 2.5cm (1in) through to a casing wide enough to take deep continental or cornice rods. The casing can be stitched with or without a heading, which sits above the rod as a frilled edging.

Lightweight short curtains made with a casing can also be supported on wire – an ideal solution for sheers in a small window or across a recess.

VALANCE OR PELMET (CORNICE)?

A pelmet or valance hides the curtain track and heading and adds a decorative finish to a window. Depending on its height and depth, a valance or pelmet can be used to alter the proportions of a window, making it look taller or shallower.

A valance is a deep frill that hangs in front of a curtain to give a soft, pretty finish to a window and, depending on the type of heading and trim used, is suitable for most rooms. Valances can be straight or shaped, and edged with braids or fringing.

In pelmets the fabric is stiffened with a backing fabric or stretched over a wooden frame. A pelmet can be straight, cut with a decorative edging, or bound or trimmed with cord, braid or fringing.

SWAGS AND TAILS

Swags and tails are a dramatic treatment for windows. The swag is a drape of fabric which hangs in front of the curtains, the tails are the elegant lengths of fabric that frame the window on either side. The more formal version is fixed to a pelmet board, but fabric can be draped informally over a curtain pole as the only form of window dressing. Although the formal swags look best on tall windows, dressing full-length curtains, they can be effective when scaled down to suit smaller windows.

▲ *Cut-out pelmet*
Here, the lower edge of the pelmet has been cleverly cut to follow the floral garland and ribbon design on the curtain fabric. The depth of the pelmet, along with drawing the curtains beyond the window on either side, visually reduces the height and narrowness of the window.

▶ *Formal swags and tails*
Elaborate swags and tails are ideal for creating a full blown window dressing. In this hallway, the window treatment takes advantage of a coordinated range of fabrics, by using a lighter version of the main curtain fabric for the swags and tails. The plain linings and tiebacks pick up on the yellow of the roses in both floral fabrics.

◀ *Informal drapes*
Choose your curtains to enhance your decorating style. Here, the plain, pale curtains hanging straight down to the floor, and swags and tails draped casually over the poles, really suit a light, minimally furnished room.

▼ *Teamwork*
Floor-length curtains with a box-headed valance make a handsome contribution to this smart living room. Details, like matching the binding and piping on the valance and tiebacks to the piped trim on the armchairs, pull the scheme together.

STRAIGHT OR WITH TIEBACKS?

Curtains that are hung straight suit a very small window, or where you want a simple style, perhaps for a cottage look or a nursery. A straight curtain can look handsome, but consider tiebacks for a more decorative or elegant finishing touch.

No-sew tieback options include using a heavy cord and elaborate tassel, or you can loop the curtains back behind metal curtain bands or holdbacks.

LINING

Lining adds insulation, protects the curtain fabric from the sun and prevents fading. It also makes your curtains drape well. For interest, use a contrast lining with a pattern or a coordinating colour. Speciality linings are available.

Interlining curtains with a soft layer of padding between the curtain fabric and lining makes them hang beautifully and gives extra insulating properties.

SHEERS AND BLINDS

One solution for problem windows, or bay or shaped windows, is to combine the curtain with a blind or separate sheer curtain.

A blind works well on windows which are covered by curtains at night, but need alternative screening from excessive sunlight or prying eyes during the day, and it can be styled to match curtains.

A sheer curtain is another answer on windows where you need to hide a view, or have daytime privacy, as it allows light to filter into the room.

11

CURTAIN ACCESSORIES

Gleaming metal and softly draped fabrics are a magical combination in a window dressing. In a traditional style, hanging the curtains from a brass pole or on metallic rings, or holding them away from the window with shiny brass knobs or brackets, called holdbacks, looks luxurious.

For the latest in simple yet exciting window treatments, contrast the richness and softness of curtain fabrics against the ruggedness of iron rods. Draping delicate sheers over a matt black iron bar is very dramatic, and well suited to a modern decorating scheme.

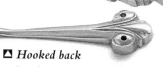

◮ Hooked back

When fixed horizontally beside a window, this moulded brass bracket is an elegant way of holding back formal curtains.

◮ Slip-on pole decorations

One solution for hanging lightweight curtains is to improvise a pole from a strip of dowel and slip ornamental rings over the ends as decoration.

◮ Scrollwork

With its end coiled into an artistic spiral, a slim iron bar makes an excellent rod for hanging a tabbed curtain.

◁ In finial style

The ornate knobs, or finials, used to decorate the ends of a curtain pole come in many shapes and materials.

◮ Hold back

A brass rosette is strong enough to hold back even a heavy curtain. You simply unhitch the fabric to draw the curtain.

◱ Hooks for tiebacks

Tiebacks restraining lightweight curtains can be looped over little brass hooks fixed to the wall or frame beside the window. Look out for pretty designs, like these leaf and floral hooks.

A Guide to Curtains

An A-Z of window treatments and the terms which are used in curtain making.

Arched edge Decorative edge shaped like an arch to rise in the middle.

Architrave (Trim) Wooden surround to window or door.
Asymmetrical curtain Curtain draped to one side of a window or of uneven length at either side of a window.

Austrian blind (balloon blind) Soft fabric blind with some fullness, gathered to form ruched swags at base.

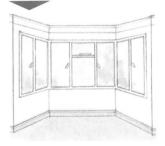

Bay window An angular projection of a house front filled by a window.

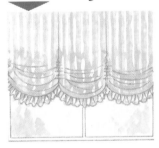

Bishop sleeve curtains Curtains with extra finished length so they billow out over tiebacks when pulled up.

Bow window A curved projection of a house front filled by a window.

Box pleats Flat pressed symmetrical pleats with fabric folded to back on both sides so adjoining side edges meet.

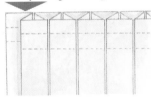

Brackets Supports for fixing curtain poles, rods and tracks to the wall.

Café curtain Curtain set on a narrow café rod halfway down the window, usually with a *slot* or *scalloped heading*.

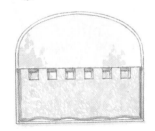

Cartridge pleats Curtain heading with rows of large cylindrical pleats.

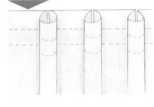

Casement curtain Curtain with a casing at top and bottom fixed on rods.

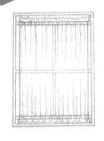

Casement window Window that opens on vertical hinges.

Castellated edge Decorative edge shaped with square indentations.

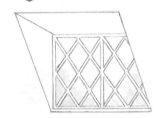

Choux rosette Decoration formed by pulling fabric through a ring into a soft pouffe resembling a cabbage (hence 'choux').

Cleats Hooked fitting beside the window to anchor blind cords when raised.
Cross-over curtains Curtains draped across a window and held back at opposite sides.

Cut drop Cut length of curtain with allowances for heading and hem turnings.

Deadlight The space between the top of the window and the ceiling.
Dormer window A small window that projects from a sloping roof.

Dress curtains Curtains which are fixed in place so they cannot be drawn.

End stop Fixture at end of track or pole to prevent gliders or rings falling off.

Fascia Thin pelmet (cornice) board covered in fabric or painted. Covers a blind or curtain heading and track.

French window A window which reaches to the floor and opens like a door to provide access to the outside.

Hold back Decorative projection in wood or metal which the curtains are tucked behind to hold them open, away from the window.

Italian stringing Method of holding a curtain open by rings and cord set diagonally across curtain width.

Festoon blind Soft fabric blind permanently gathered into shallow swags that run down the whole length of the blind.

Finial Decorative *end-stop* on curtain pole.

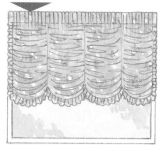

Finished length Length of a finished curtain.
Flemish heading *Goblet pleats* trimmed with rope or furnishing cord, looped and knotted at base of pleats.

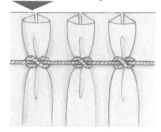

French pleats (pinch pleats) Hand-sewn *triple pleat* curtain heading in which three folds of fabric are pinched together.

Fullness Additional length or width of fabric to allow for drapes, gathers, pleats or swags in a curtain.

Gathered heading Basic gathered heading formed by a narrow heading tape.

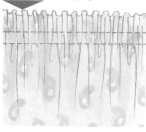

Gliders Runners that fit into and slide along the curtain track to carry curtains.

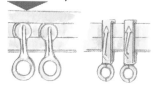

Goblet pleats Formal curtain heading of large cylindrical pleats pinched at the base to form goblet shapes.

Half drop With diagonal patterns allow half the pattern drop as the repeat.
Heading tape Tape attached to the curtain which pulls up to form gathers or pleats.
Hem weight Lead weight sewn into the curtain hem and seams to prevent the curtain puckering at the seams.

Hook drop Measurement from the eye of the curtain hook to the floor.
Hour-glass curtain A *casement curtain* held taut on a rod at top and bottom, and drawn in at the centre forming an hour-glass shape.

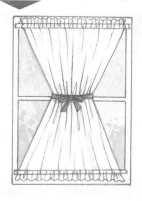

Interlining Soft layer between curtain fabric and lining to give weight and substance, provide insulation, and block light and noise.
Inverted pleat (kick pleat) Reversed *box pleat* with edges of pleat meeting in middle on right side of fabric.

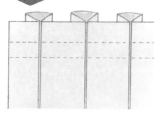

Inverted scallop edge Decorative edge shaped with half-circle indentations.

Lambrequin A stiff, shaped surround to a window, continuing down the sides of the frame.

Lath and fascia Arrangement of *pelmet lath*, *fascia* and *track* which allows heading to be visible but conceals track when curtains are open.

Leading edge Edge of curtain facing into centre of window.
Lead-weighted tape Small lead weights slotted into a tape, used to weight the hems of fine fabrics.
Lining Layer of fabric sewn to the back of curtain to protect it from light, improve insulation and way it hangs.
London blind (flat blind) Soft fabric blind that when raised has a loose swag effect at the base.

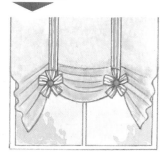

Maltese cross rosette A decorative feature formed by two loops of fabric pressed flat and placed across each other at right angles then secured together.

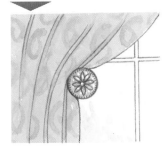

Ombra (embrace) A decorative projection in wood or metal used for holding curtains to the side of the window.

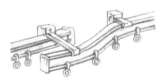

Overlap The point where the curtains meet and cross over by approximately 7.5cm (3in) in the middle of the track or pole.

Oversail The amount by which a pole or track extends on either side beyond the width of the window.

Pattern repeat The distance covered by a fabric design before it repeats itself, usually measured on the length for estimating purposes.

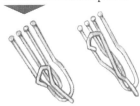

Pelmet (cornice) A decorative surround to conceal curtain *track* and *heading*; can be flat and shaped, often attached to a pelmet box. Alternatively, it is a soft *valance* gathered on to a pole or track.

Pencil pleats A tape or hand sewn curtain heading formed by vertical rows of narrow, densely packed folds.

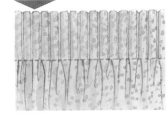

Picture window A large window with wide panes of glass usually placed so that it overlooks a view.

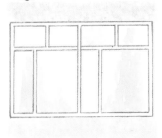

Pin hooks S-shaped curtain hooks with sharpened end for pushing into curtain heading.
Pinch pleats See *French pleats*.
Plastic-covered wire Wire cased in plastic with hooks or screw eyes at the ends to support a lightweight slot-headed curtain.

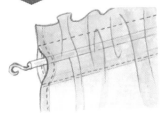

Pleated rosette Decorative feature formed by tightly and evenly pleating a band of fabric into a circular fan shape.

Pleater hooks Curtain hooks used with a cordless heading tape in which the forks of the hook fit into slots in the tape to form the curtain pleats.

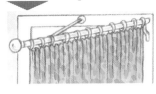

Pole A sturdy wooden, metal or plastic bar used with curtain rings to hang medium to heavyweight curtains.

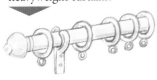

Portière rod A rod to hold a curtain at an external door, with a hinged end that lifts up as the door is opened.

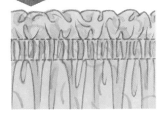

Puffball heading A deep stand-up at the top of a curtain, which is puffed up.

Reefing line A row of rings sewn to the back of a curtain or blind which carries the cord to raise or lower the curtain.

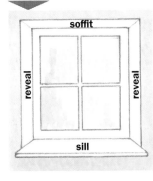

Return The sides of a curtain, valance or pelmet which project out at right angles to the wall.
Reveal The depth of a wall or window frame recess on each side of a window.

soffit

reveal

reveal

sill

Rod A narrow metal or plastic bar used to hang lighter weight curtains.

Roller blind A flat shade that rolls up around a cylinder at the top of the window.

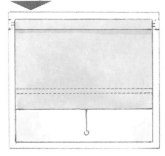

Roman blind Corded blind with base rod and sometimes more rods set horizontally across the back forming straight folds when blind is pulled up.

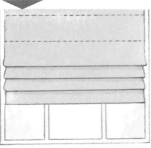

Rose A decorative feature formed by gathering and twisting fabric to form a rose-like shape.

Sail blind A flat fabric shade secured to the window frame at all four corners with screw-in hooks and eyelets.
Sash window A window with a vertically sliding frame rather than hinges.

Scalloped edge A decorative edge, shaped with regular semicircular protrusions.

Scalloped heading The scalloped top edge of a curtain with rings or hooks attached to the scallops.

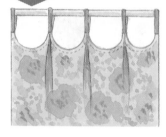

Self-adhesive fabric stiffener Iron-on pelmet interfacing used to stiffen fabric.

Serpentine edge A decorative edge shaped with wavy curves.

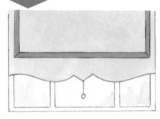

Sew-on hooks Traditional curtain hooks sewn on to gathered or pleated headings.

Sheer curtains/blinds Translucent window dressing made of very lightweight, opaque fabric which provides privacy without blocking light.

Sill A horizontal ledge at base of window (see *Reveal*)

Sky light A window set into a roof or ceiling to provide overhead lighting.

Slot heading (case heading) A stitched, tube-like heading at the top edge of a curtain, which the rod or pole is pushed through.

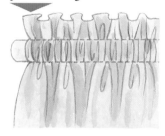

Soffit The upper plane of a window opening, at right-angles to the wall, above the window (see *Reveal*).

Smocked heading A *pencil pleat heading* stitched to create a honeycomb effect.

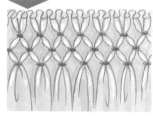

Spring clips Decorative curtain rings to thread over rods or poles, with clip attachments that grip the top edge of light or sheer curtains.

Stand-up The part of the curtain extending above the *suspension point*.

Suspension point The line along top edge of the curtain, below which the fabric is hanging (see *Stand-up*).

Swag A length of fabric which has been arranged to hang in sweeping folds above a window or bed.

Tab headings An open curtain heading in which the curtain hangs below a pole or rod suspended by fabric loops or ties.

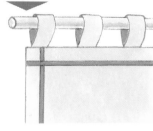

Tail Folded or pleated fabric arranged to fall in vertical folds between or at the ends of *swags* (see *Swag*).

Tension rod A fine plastic rod with an internal spring mechanism to hold it in place across the window recess, often used for café curtains.

Thermal lining Interlining with an insulating aluminium backing.

Tie-back A shaped and stiffened band, plait, tasselled cord etc, to hold curtains to the side of a window.

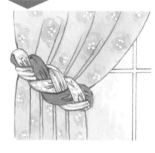

Track A plastic or metal curtain rail with fitted *gliders*.

Trefoil A double pleat used for accent in a valance.

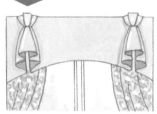

Triple pleats See *French pleats*.

Trumpet A conical pleat used for accent in a valance.

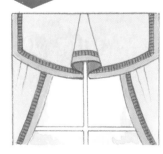

Tudor ruff heading A curtain heading with a tightly gathered, smocked shape.

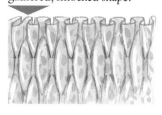

Unlined curtain A single thickness curtain that does not block out too much light.

Valance A soft fabric pelmet with a gathered or flat skirt hanging at the top of the window to conceal the track.

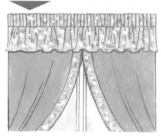

Valance rail A fixture projecting from the front of either a curtain track or pole to carry a *valance* in front of the curtain.

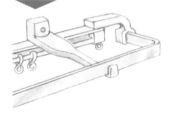

Vogue heading A curtain heading with staggered pinched pleats.

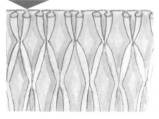

Zigzag A decorative edge cut into sharp triangular-shaped points.

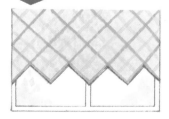

Fabrics for dressing windows

Fabrics should be chosen for their practical qualities as well as for their visual appeal.

Windows are the natural light source and a focal point in any room, so it's important to take some time deciding on the window treatment for the look you want to achieve. You should consider all the practical points listed below before you make a final fabric selection.

Functions of a window dressing

Filtering light An unlined curtain or blind hanging in front of a window during the day diffuses sunlight shining into the room.

Blocking light Lined and interlined window dressings made in closely woven fabrics prevent light from entering the room, prevent fading of other soft furnishings, and help you to sleep.

Excluding draughts Curtains made in a dense, heavyweight fabric with a pile or fluffy texture, such as velvet or tweed, or in a lighter fabric with a thermal lining, help to reduce draughts and insulate a room.

Privacy Sheer curtains or blinds are a good idea if you need to conceal an ugly outlook or if you want to safeguard your privacy as they block the view, while still letting in some light.

Reducing sound Densely woven fabrics, with an absorptive, spongy texture, are best at muffling sounds.

The nature of the fabric

You can use almost any type of fabric to dress a window – there are no hard and fast rules. Some of the best effects come from using fabrics in an unusual way.

Drapability It is essential to know how a fabric hangs, as this dictates the final look of the curtains. Hold up a bolt of fabric, let some hang down and note how it drapes.

Texture and weight Feel the fabric and make a mental note of its texture and weight. Bunch up or fold a corner of the fabric to see how it gathers or pleats.

Care considerations

Choose fabrics that can withstand the amount of washing or handling you expect them to receive. Remember that some fabrics, such as chintz, may lose their finish when washed. Curtains in kitchens and bathrooms, or those hanging at windows near a busy road, need regular laundering to keep them fresh, so machine washable fabrics or ones with a stain retardant finish are most suitable.

Linings

Adding a lining is an extra expense but an investment too, if it helps to eliminate light or draughts. A lining also protects silk and linen fabrics and other interior soft furnishings from the damaging effects of sunlight.

Decide on the lining at the same time as you buy the fabric to ensure that the two fabrics are compatible in weight and laundering properties. Check that your chosen lining gives the curtains adequate body and protection; if they need extra weight, buy some curtain interlining.

Blinds

Blinds are usually made from stiffer fabrics that do not require draping qualities.

Roman blinds are best made from closely woven cloth, such as chintz, cretonne, or sateen, which pleats or folds well.

Roller blinds require similar, closely woven fabrics. Alternatively, you can buy stiffened fabric especially for roller blinds which is woven in a range of widths.

Austrian and **festoon blinds** require a fabric such as chintz, cotton or cotton sateen. This makes them sturdy enough to pleat well but light enough to be gathered up into swags or on to a curtain heading.

Cost factors

It is false economy to skimp on the quality or quantity of fabric – scanty curtains do not drape or move well. Instead choose a style and fabric within your budget. Simple blinds or tab-headed curtains take less fabric than fuller styles, while many inexpensive fabrics, such as muslin and calico, make impressive curtains.

It can also be worth looking in the dressmaking fabrics section. Many are perfectly suitable for lightweight curtains – gingham, dotted voile, even plaids can be used as window dressings.

WAYS OF REDUCING COSTS

Use a cheaper fabric, but maintain a luxurious look by extending the curtain drop so it sits on the floor, and increasing the gathering allowance.

❖

Make window dressings that require less fabric – blinds or tab-headed curtains

❖

Make an informal window dressing using a table cloth, piece of lace or sarong.

❖

Choose a plain fabric or one with a small pattern repeat, because matching patterns uses extra fabric.

❖

Check the fabric width – you may be able to buy fabric wide enough to avoid joining so many widths, or use a wide-width fabric sideways for a blind.

❖

If you are using a heading tape, certain types gather less fabric – check on the heading tape box for gathering allowance.

Properties of fabrics

* May be hard to find in the USA

Fabric	Heavy	Medium	Light	Filters Light	Blocks Light	Excludes draughts	Reduces sound	Drapes well	Pleats well	Gathers well	Easy care
Brocade	▬	▬			✦	✦	✦	✦			
BroderieAnglaise*			▬	✦						✦	✦
Calico		▬	▬						✦		✦
Chintz		▬						✦	✦	✦	
Corduroy	▬	▬			✦	✦	✦	✦			
Cotton		▬	▬	✦					✦	✦	✦
Cretonne		▬			✦			✦	✦		✦
Crewelwork*	▬	▬		✦		✦		✦			
Damask		▬						✦	✦		
Dobby*		▬			✦				✦		
Dotted Swiss			▬	✦				✦		✦	✦
Dupion*		▬						✦		✦	
Gingham		▬	▬	✦						✦	✦
Hessian	▬	▬		✦							✦
Holland		▬							✦		
Lace			▬	✦				✦		✦	
Lawn*			▬	✦					✦	✦	✦
Linen Union*		▬						✦	✦		✦
Moire		▬				✦		✦			
Muslin			▬	✦				✦		✦	
Net			▬	✦					✦	✦	✦
Sateen		▬				✦	✦	✦	✦		
Satin		▬				✦	✦	✦	✦		
Seersucker		▬	▬	✦						✦	✦
Shantung			▬	✦				✦		✦	
Tapestry	▬	▬			✦	✦	✦	✦			
Tweed	▬	▬			✦	✦		✦			
Velvet	▬	▬			✦	✦	✦	✦			
Voile			▬	✦				✦		✦	

Making curtains

Precise measuring up and cutting out are the crucial first steps to sewing curtains that hang well.

Your choice of curtain style will depend largely on the size and shape of your window, other soft furnishings in the room and the visual effect you want to create. This guide to measuring up can be used for all straight-fall, fabric curtains, lined or unlined, made with tape headings. (Available by the metre or yard from fabric departments, heading tapes are attached to the top of the curtains as the quickest and easiest way of pleating and hanging them.)

You need the following information to calculate the total fabric required to make curtains for a window:

♦ **The width of the curtain track or pole**
♦ **The finished gathered width of each curtain**
♦ **The fabric requirement of the curtain heading tape**
♦ **The desired curtain length**
♦ **The pattern repeat**

Curtain track or pole

Before measuring up for curtains, fix the track or pole you plan to use in place so that its exact height and width can be measured. As a guide, fix the track or pole between 7.5-12.5cm (3-5in) above the window and allow at least 15cm (6in) overlap on each side, unless it is in a recess, so that the curtain can be swept back away from the window to let in maximum light.

Curtain width

First, simply measure the length of the track or pole and divide this measurement by two for a pair of curtains. For certain tracks, you will have to add extra fabric for an overlap between the two curtains in the centre, so check the instructions with the track.

Heading tape

Now, choose the heading tape you want to use – you will need to know this before you can work out the final fabric amounts because the gathering allowance for different styles of heading tape varies, as the chart to the right shows. As a general guide, you will need at least 1½-2 times the width of the curtain to achieve the necessary fullness.

Curtain length

There are three popular curtain lengths:

Sill length (A) – the curtain hems are 1cm (⅜in) above the sill so that they sweep clear of it.

Below the sill (B) – the curtains hang best if they are between 10 and 15cm (4-6in) below the sill.

Floor length (C) – the curtain hems are 1cm (⅜in) above the floor to prevent wear.

For the curtain length, measure from the top of the fixed curtain track, or from the base of the rings on the curtain pole, to the desired position of the lower edge of the curtain. Ignore heading seam and hem allowances at this stage; they are added on later when calculating fabric quantity.

Measure to top of track if track is fitted
Measure to base of rings if a pole is fitted

Heading tape	Fabric needed		
Standard tape	1½-2	x	
Pencil pleat tape	2½-3	x	
Triple pleat	2	x	Gathered
Cartridge pleat	2	x	curtain
Box pleat	3	x	width
Goblet pleat	2	x	
Smocked tape	2	x	

This curtain is gathered using a pencil pleat tape. The ungathered fabric was 2½ -3 times wider than its finished gathered width.

Pattern repeat

For patterned fabrics, you will need to buy extra so that you can match up the pattern across the width and when the curtains are drawn together. Make allowances, too, for any overlap between the closed curtains. To work out the extra fabric required, you have to know the pattern repeat.

To find the pattern repeat allowance, measure the distance (**R**) along the selvedge edge between one pattern motif and the same point on the next identical one. This is often quoted on furnishing fabric details, so look out for it when you are choosing the fabric. As a general guideline, add one extra pattern repeat for every fabric width required.

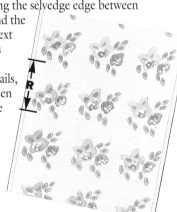

Calculating fabric quantity

The chart below shows how to work out the total amount of fabric needed. The example given here is for curtains, 2m (6⅝ft) long, with a triple pleat tape heading; fill in the blank parts of the chart to calculate the amount of fabric you will need to make curtains for your window. You may find a pocket calculator helpful.

Make sure you always use accurate measurements and measure up all windows separately even if they look identical.

Loosening up

Only work with full and half fabric widths. If your calculations fall the odd bit over a convenient width, ease off the gathering on the heading tape slightly, rather than add another half width of the fabric.

Curtain length	Example cm	in	Your window cm	in
Length of each curtain	200	80		
+ Hem (for 7.5cm/3in deep hem)	12.5	5	12.5	5
+ Heading seam	1.5	⅝	1.5	⅝
+ Pattern repeat	40	16		
Total cut length	**254**	**101⅝**		

Curtain width	cm	in	cm	in
Gathered width of each curtain	85	34		
x Allowance for gathering (see heading tape chart)	2			
+ Side hems	10	4	10	4
* Total width for each curtain (add overlap allowance if applicable)	180	72		
÷ Sold fabric width	122	48		
So Number of fabric widths per curtain needed		1½		
x Number of curtains		2		
= Total number of widths		**3**		

Total fabric needed				
Total cut length	254	102		
x Total number of widths		3		
= Total fabric length	762	306		
SO BUY:	**7.8m**	**8½yd**		

* Note: If you need more than one full fabric width to make up the ungathered curtain width, remember to include extra seam allowances.

Cutting out

Find a large flat surface – a clean floor is ideal – that will take the complete curtain length and width. For matching patterned fabrics, you also need to be able to lay two widths side by side.

1 Preparing to cut Lay the fabric flat, right side up. On patterned fabrics, plan, then mark the position of the base; for the best effect, the complete pattern, or a clear section of it, should sit along the base of the curtain after the hem has been turned up.

2 Straightening up the base edge Use a ring binder or a large set/L square to mark the base edge at right angles out from the selvedge. Then cut the fabric along the marked line.

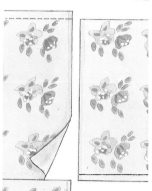

3 Cutting out Measure the curtain length up from the base edge and, again using your binder or a large set/L square and ruler, mark the top edge and cut along it. To cut the second length, place the uncut fabric against the cut length and match any pattern design across the two pieces. Cut remaining lengths in the same way.

Joining widths

You may need to join lengths of fabric together to make the total ungathered width for each curtain. If the curtain contains full widths and a half, place the half width on the outer edge.

1 Joining widths Pin the fabric widths together, right sides facing, and then look on the right side to check that the pattern matches. To be sure of an exact match, hold the lengths together using ladder stitch.

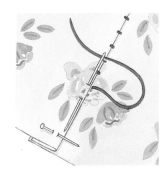

2 Stitching widths Machine stitch the widths together taking a 1.5cm (⅝in) seam allowance. Press the seams to one side, trim to 6mm (¼in), then neaten them with zigzag stitch and remove any ladder stitching. Alternatively, for unlined curtains you can use a French seam.

TIP

The pattern repeat on some fabrics can be quite large, so after cutting out your curtain widths use spare pieces of fabric to make matching tiebacks or scatter cushions.

Hemming curtains

A neatly turned, even hem is crucial to the appearance of your curtains.

There are several ways of turning the hem, depending on whether the curtains are unlined or lined and the kind of fabric used. However, a few general rules apply to most methods:

❖ Allow a double hem. This will make the curtain hang better. Only use a single hem for an interlined curtain.

❖ Turn up the hem on the grain. If it is slightly off grain it will distort. To prevent this, ensure that you cut out the curtains on the fabric grain.

❖ To help prevent seams puckering, which will lift the hem at the seam, use a long stitch for the seams and clip into all selvedges at intervals of 8-10cm (3-4in).

❖ Keep the fabric well supported while pressing the hem. Try pinning the curtain to the ironing board pad in a few places to prevent it slipping. Alternatively, spread a sheet on the floor, lay the curtain out flat on top, then press up the hem.

❖ Use the appropriate curtain weight inserted in the hem to help the curtains hang well, and prevent the seams puckering.

❖ Let the curtains hang for a few days before stitching the hem. Always double check the length of the curtains before the final stitching.

Hem stitching

Curtain hems can be held with hand stitches, machine straight or blind stitches, or be fused in place, depending on the curtain style, the desired finish and how much time you want to spend.

Hand stitching Use flat hemming or hemming slipstitch (see page 64).

Fusing Cut fusible web tape (Bondaweb) to match the length of the hem. Press in place, following the manufacturer's instructions for the temperature setting on the iron and times.

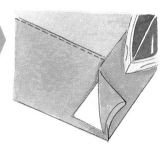

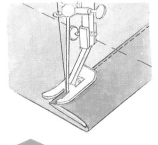

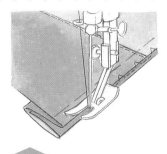

Machine straight stitching To allow bulky hems to feed easily through the machine, lessen the foot pressure. Stitch close to the folded hem edge using a medium length straight stitch.

Machine blindstitch Turn hem fold to right side, leaving 3mm (⅛in) extending, and tack. Set machine to blindstitch, and position fabric so the stitch catches in only a few threads of curtain.

Adding curtain weights

There are two types of weight: small metal disks rather like buttons, and covered chain weights, also known as lead weight tape. Both are sold by fabric or furnishing departments and are available in different weights. As a guide, match the curtain weight to the weight of the curtain fabric and length of the curtain.

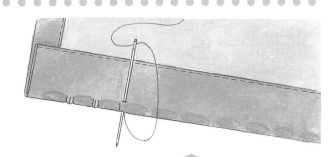

Metal disk weights Use the metal disks for full length curtains made in medium to heavyweight fabrics to prevent the curtains from puckering at the seams.

Most weights have holes which allow them to be stitched in place like a button.

On lined curtains, position the weight on the finished hem so that it is hidden by the lining.

On unlined curtains, stitch the weight into the side seam or hide it in a small pocket of fabric.

Making a pocket From a scrap of curtain fabric, cut two squares to cover the weight, plus 6mm (¼in) seam. With right sides together, stitch round three sides and turn back to the right side. Insert the weight, fold in the edges and slipstitch the opening closed. Attach the pocket in the corner of the curtain over the seams.

Chain weights Covered chain weights are inserted along the entire hem length of light or sheer curtains to help them hang well and prevent them from billowing.

Adding chain weights Insert a length of chain weight through the hem, within the first fold. Trim to just less than the curtain width, then catch in place at side edges, any seams and a few points in between with a few hand stitches.

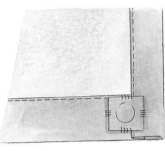

Double hem on unlined curtains

For a professional finish, stitch the side hems after the lower hem. With this method the weight can be inserted into the side seam. Alternatively, it can be attached in a pocket of fabric. If you do not want the stitching to show on the right side, use machine blindstitch or a hand slipstitch.

1 **Turning up the hem** Turn under and press 7.5cm (3in) on the lower edge. Then press under another 7.5cm (3in). Stitch the hem.

2 **Sewing side hems** Turn under and press a double 2.5cm (1in) hem on each side edge. Sew a weight to the lower hem, just under the side hem fold, then stitch the side hem in place.

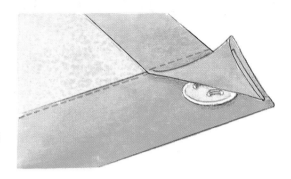

Curtains with machine-stitched lining

Make up the curtains so that the lining edge lies 12.5cm (5in) above the raw edge of the curtain fabric. When stitching the curtain and lining side edges together, end the stitching approximately 23cm (9in) from the bottom edge of the curtain fabric. See page 43 for more information on making lined curtains.

1 **Hemming the lining** Turn under and press the free side edges of the lining. Turn under and press a double 2.5cm (1in) hem on the lower edge of the lining. Tack then machine stitch lining hem and press.

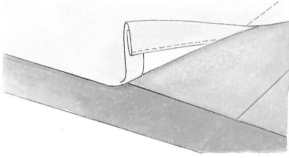

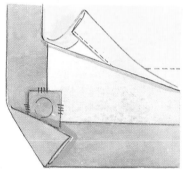

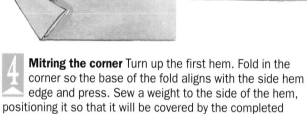

4 **Mitring the corner** Turn up the first hem. Fold in the corner so the base of the fold aligns with the side hem edge and press. Sew a weight to the side of the hem, positioning it so that it will be covered by the completed hem. Turn up the final hem.

2 **Turning up the curtain hem** Fold up and press a 5cm (2in) hem on the lower edge of the curtain. Then turn up the hem again by 7.5cm (3in) and pin. Carefully supporting the curtain on an ironing board, or laying it out flat on the floor, press the hem.

3 **Reducing the bulk** Open out the curtain hem folds and cut away part of the side hem allowance on the first fold, leaving about 6mm (¼in) on the edge.

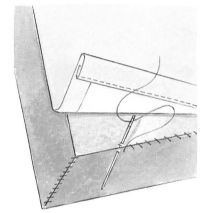

5 **Stitching hem** Tack then hem by hand, using flat hemming stitch, including the mitred corners.

6 **Finishing lining** Neatly hand slipstitch the free side edges of the lining to the sides of the curtain.

7 **Working a bar tack** To hold the lining and curtain hems together, work a couple of bar tacks along the overlap. Fasten the thread to the curtain hem, under the lining. Work four stitches alternately in the lining and curtain hems, leaving 2-3cm (¾-1¼in) of thread between each stitch. Work buttonhole stitch closely over the threads. Fasten off.

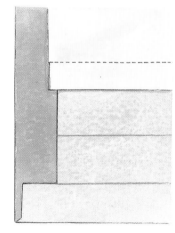

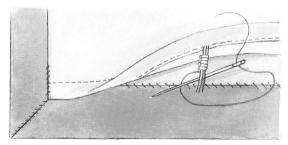

> ### ▼▼▼ T I P ▼▼▼
> **CARD GAUGE**
> To ensure even turnings, cut a 40cm (16in) strip of cardboard to the required depth, and fold the fabric over the strip when pressing.

Heading tapes

A well chosen heading tape adds a final flourish to your curtains.

Ready-made heading tapes are the easiest way of gathering the top of a curtain or valance. The tapes are available in different styles and depths, and are stitched flat to the top of the curtain or valance. They have cords threaded through them, and when the cords are pulled up, neat gathers or pleats (depending on the tape style) are formed.

Other types of curtain headings are dealt with on pages 25–26.

TIP

ADJUSTING WIDTHS
The final width of your curtains can be varied greatly by making the pleats or gathers more or less tight. However, with triple and cylindrical pleats there is less flexibility for altering the width of the curtain.

What heading tape?

The choice of heading tape depends on your own preference and the style of curtain required. **Traditional style** heading tapes which are readily available include gathered; pencil pleated; box pleated; triple pleated and cylindrical. Of these gathered, pencil pleated and triple pleated are sold in a choice of three different depths. There are also special tapes for sheer and net curtains. These are made in lightweight, almost translucent material. Three **novelty styles,** vogue, smocked and Tudor ruff, are also quite widely sold.

As a general guideline, relate the depth of the tape to the length of the curtain – deep heading tapes (triple pleated and cylindrical) are best suited to long formal curtains. Tapes sold in narrow depths (gathered or pencil pleated) work for shorter or sill length curtains.

Heading tapes have pockets or loops designed to take the curtain hooks. Each style of tape requires its own specific hook – check the manufacturer's instructions.

The type of hook will also depend on how you want to hang the curtain – with most tapes the hooks can be positioned in different levels on the tape to allow the curtain to be hung either from a pole or up over a curtain track. However, some of the triple pleated tapes can be hung in only one way – always check the manufacturer's instructions on the packet carefully before buying.

What fabric?

All the tapes are suitable for most fabrics although, again, try and marry the tape to the fabric – for instance a simple gathered heading would be best with a light unlined cotton curtain, while a triple or cylindrical pleat would suit heavy velvet. Plain fabrics benefit from a very decorative heading tape, while a print may require only a simple style.

Check the weight and drapability of the fabric too: a heavy fabric does not gather up well into pencil pleats but suits the drama of cylindrical pleats. A fabric that hangs well – such as a mediumweight shantung – suits triple pleats, which release the fabric into deep folds, while a very light flimsy fabric, such as voile, is best gathered.

Tapes can be laundered or drycleaned, so follow the care instructions for the curtain fabric when laundering the finished curtains.

Tape and fabric amounts

The different headings require different amounts of fabric. As a guide: gathered headings need 1½ times the track width of fabric; box and pencil pleats take 2½ times the track width; triple and cylindrical pleats need 3 times. For sheer or net curtains allow at least 2 times the track width.

You will need the same amount of tape as the total flat width of all the curtains, plus extra for finishing the tape ends and placing pleats – allow about 34cm (⅜yd) extra per curtain.

For more information on fabric amounts see pages 19–20.

Linings

There are tapes available for making detachable linings. These gather up the lining heading separately. The curtain hooks catch both the lining and the main fabric to the pole or track.

For curtains which have attached linings, make up the curtain with its lining first, then add the heading tape of your choice.

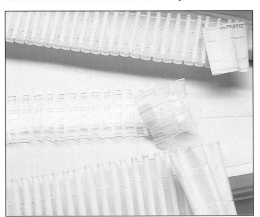

▶ *A vogue heading tape, one of several novelty styles, gathers the curtain fabric into a very elegant effect. A deep tape such as this is best suited to long, formal curtains.*

Gripping tapes

The newest style of heading tape works without a track or pole – it simply sticks to an adhesive strip that is pressed on to a wall. It is ideal for curtains that do not need to be drawn, windows that are an awkward shape or pelmets. The actual heading tape is stitched to the curtain top in the usual way.

Traditional style tapes

Gathered pleat

This tape is suitable for all fabrics and produces a simple, attractive heading that's ideal for informal or country style curtains. *You need fabric 1½ times the curtain track width.*

Pencil pleat

Suitable for most settings, this heading tape gives a neat, elegant look to curtains. It comes in different depths to match the curtain lengths and weights – deeper headings will give a better proportion on longer curtains. *You need fabric 2½ times the track width.*

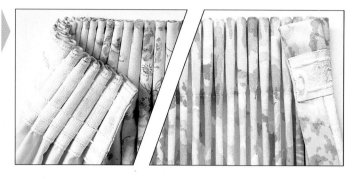

Box pleat

A formal heading tape, box pleats emphasize the curtain length. The pleats show up well on plain fabrics; they are also ideal for valances on chairs, settees and dressing tables. *You need fabric 2½ times the track width.*

Cylindrical pleat

This is a good choice for curtains in heavier fabrics or interlined curtains. Take care to match the pleats across the centre opening unless curtains overlap. *You need fabric 3 times the track width.*

Sheers

There are a couple of heading tapes suitable for very lightweight lace or sheer curtains. The tapes are made in a light mesh material – the one shown here gathers the curtain up into pencil pleats. *You need fabric 2 times the track width.*

Triple pleat

This heading tape makes the curtain drape well and it is available in three different depths. It is best for mediumweight fabrics. Position the tape so that the pleats fall evenly across the curtains with equal space at each end. *You need fabric 3 times the track width.*

Novelty style tapes

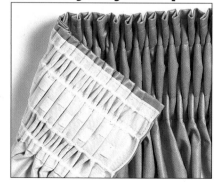

Tudor ruff

This type of heading is a decorative alternative to the pencil pleat and is ideal for jazzing up plain fabrics. *You need fabric 2 times the track width.*

Smocked

This effect was once the craft of the professional curtain maker. It is extremely decorative and looks good on both plain and patterned fabrics. It is particularly popular on nets and sheers. *You need fabric 2 times the track width.*

Vogue

Similar to a Tudor ruff heading, this tape gives a stylish and elegant effect. *You need fabric 2 times the track width.*

NO-SEW WINDOW HEADINGS

With some crafty draping and a little ingenuity, you can create lovely festooned headings for your windows from lengths of fabric or garlands of dried flowers – all without sewing a stitch.

A graceful swag and tails heading frames a window beautifully. That wonderful, just-thrown-over-the-pole look seems so effortless; generous swoops of fabric or flowers simply twined over a pole or looped across from side to side become the window's crowning glory. The really clever part is that these headings stay in place while remaining so casually draped. This calls for some invisible trickery in the shape of tacks, staples or Velcro fastening to stop the twists and loops of the swags unfurling. You avoid any sewing by tucking selvedges into the drapes and knotting off fraying raw ends. Look for pieces of fabric that are already trimmed with binding, fringing or lace; tablecloths, shawls, sheers, bedspreads and light throws are all likely candidates.

Showy and pretty rather than practical, these headings work best on curtainless windows with lovely views, or in conjunction with blinds or fixed sheers. In summer, a light heading is the perfect substitute for heavy curtains.

To create an attractive draped heading like this, you simply wind the fabric through special coiled holdbacks called valance creators.

A floral garland makes the most of a window with a good view. Here a sweetly scented garland, tied up with fabric bows to match the paintwork, gives this little window a cottagey appearance.

Simple devices, like these ring clips, are great for putting up quick headings. The snap-shut grips firmly hold a strip of sheer fabric to create a frilly window topping.

These small clips are ideal for holding lightweight sheer fabrics. You can also get larger, stronger clips for carrying heavier fabrics on thicker poles.

Draping fabric over a curtain pole creates a truly impressive window dressing. Here the full length tails fall behind the pole with a deep swag in front. They are held in place with tacks along the back of the pole.

IMPROVISED DRAPES

Capture a moment of creative spontaneity with window dressings styled by improvising fabric drapes and fixtures. Definitive looks can vary from the unashamedly dramatic to low-key and casual.

Besides exuding creative flair and a certain style confidence, improvised drapes offer any reluctant curtain maker a perfect opportunity to create impressive window treatments that belie the quick-and-easy methods involved – you can achieve some draped effects without sewing a single stitch. As cross-over and other improvised drapes are usually fixed styles, which can't be opened and closed, they do not require curtain heading tape and hooks or other conventional fixings. This opens the way for a choice of unusual design possibilities.

Inexpensive fabrics such as lightweight cottons, muslin and sheers come into their own for this style of window dressing. Not only do they drape well and look good, but you can use them as a foundation layer for valance effects, trimmings, and other finishing touches using more costly fabrics. In the same way, firmer natural fabrics such as calico or hessian are good basics.

Woven checks and stripes have no definite right or wrong side or pattern direction, making them and other fabrics which look good both ways round ideal for informal draped arrangements.

Many ready-made household linens can also be an inspired choice for improvised drapes. Lace and embroidered tablecloths, bedspreads and throws, or exotic saris and shawls are all possibilities. The beauty of this approach is that you can often put the fabrics back to their original use, as they needn't be cut or joined.

Plain white bed sheets provide a low-key yet elegant window dressing in this bedroom where the style note is classic simplicity. The improvised drapes are attached by curtain rings to a row of tieback hooks spaced across the window frame. Sweeping the drapes up to a hook at each side of the window lets in the light during the day.

27

MAKING CROSS-OVER DRAPES

The cross-over drapes here are made by joining together two separate drapes along the top edge so they hang as one unit. Cross-over drapes cover a large part of the window, so some resulting light loss is a consideration, though you can keep this to a minimum by choosing a sheer or semi-sheer fabric. For a subtle effect, combine toning colour fabrics for each drape as in the room shown on the right, or introduce soft pattern elements with printed voiles. Or, for speed and simplicity, bed sheets may be wide enough to create cross-over drapes without the need for joining fabric widths.

For the best effect, allow for both fabric lengths to stretch right across the window, from one side to the other, so they drape back to create two generously curved swags. To compensate for the fullness of the curve on each draped edge, you can cut the fabric so that this edge is longer than the straight side edge, as shown in the steps; this means the base hems will hang level when the drapes are caught back at the sides of the window with a tieback or metal holdback. Without this shaping, the pulled-back edges are raised and shortened into soft tails – also

an attractive option, but one that works better on narrow windows than on wide ones.

IMPROVISED FIXINGS

Decorative curtain tieback hooks, and stylish, designer-inspired screw-in knobs and handles which strike a contemporary note are ideal for improvised fixings for all kinds of drapes, as are more traditional brass or iron, post-style curtain holdbacks. More unusual fixings could be a wooden Shaker peg rail for an American country-style look, or heavy duty hooks, nails or screws for radical minimalism. Depending on the style of the window, any of these fixings can be positioned across the frame or secured to a batten outside the reveal.

To hang the drapes in place, you can either use loops of cotton tape, fancy braid or ribbon – fix these at one end with touch-and-close tape so that they can be opened to pass over large knobs, holdbacks or chunky pegs; or use small curtain rings, which suit the scale of small hooks.

YOU WILL NEED

- ❖ BATTEN AND FIXINGS (optional)
- ❖ KNOB OR HOOK FIXINGS for the drapes
- ❖ TAPE MEASURE, PENCIL
- ❖ TWO HOLDBACKS for the window sides
- ❖ STRING
- ❖ FABRIC
- ❖ PINS, SCISSORS
- ❖ COTTON TAPE and TOUCH-AND-CLOSE TAPE (VELCRO) or CURTAIN RINGS

---

1 Estimating for fixings Fit a batten over the window if required, securing it with screws into wallplugs. Screw in one of your chosen fixings at each end of the frame or batten. Decide how many fixings will lie in-between; this affects the drape of the fabric along the top edge – widely spaced fixings and generous fabric fullness create deep scallops, while closer set fixings and narrower drapes give more of a pleat effect.

2 Fitting the fixings Measure between the two end fixings on the frame or batten, and divide this measurement by one less than the total number of fixings you wish to use. Mark the fixing points on the frame or batten and screw the fixings in place. Fit the holdbacks for the sides of the window in position at the desired height.

3 Measuring up Measure the window width (**A**), and multiply by 1½ or 2 depending how full you want the drapes to be. Measure the side edge of the window from one corner fixing to the floor (**B**), and add 15cm (6in) for hems. Tie a length of string to the fixing on the opposite side of the window and drape it over the holdback on the other side and down to the ground (**C**); measure it and add 15cm (6in) for hems.

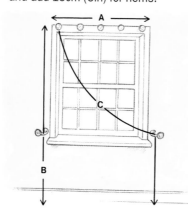

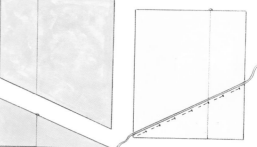

4 Shaping the base hem Join fabric widths as necessary to make up two pieces to the required width by the longest length measurement **C** including hem allowance. On the right side of one fabric piece, measure and mark **B** plus the hem allowance down from the top edge. Lay a length of string from this mark to the opposite base corner, and pin along it. Cut along the pin line. Repeat for the other fabric piece.

5 Making up Turn in and stitch a narrow hem at the side edges of each drape. Lay the drapes one over the other, with right sides up, so the long edges are on opposite sides. Stitch the drapes along the top edge. Turn top drape to the back to enclose seam. Press.

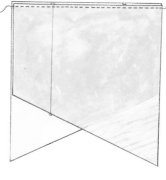

7 Attaching the hanging loops or rings

Loops: Loop a tape measure over one of the fixings, and use this measurement as a guide to cut a length of cotton tape for each loop. Sew one end of each tape to a pin mark on the drapes' wrong side, stitching through the seam allowances for strength, but not through to the right side. Stitch a small piece of touch-and-close tape to the free end of each cotton tape, and a corresponding piece firmly to the drape, next to the stitched tape end.

Rings: Stitch a curtain ring to the drapes at each pin mark as above, halfway or fully below the top edge.

8 Hanging the drapes

Starting at one end, pass each loop round a fixing and press together the fastening tapes; or slip the curtain rings over the fixings. Sweep each drape back behind a holdback and distribute the folds evenly.

☑ *A lace bedspread becomes a pretty curtain, suspended with shiny ring clips. The folded top edge forms a graceful valance.*

▲ *Cross-over drapes in toning semi-sheers make a stylish and effective filter for strong sunlight in this restful bedroom. As the drapes cover most of the window area, they're best used in sunny locations where light will still penetrate. They're also a good choice for overlooked rooms and windows with unattractive outlooks.*

6 Marking hanging positions

Measure across the top of the drapes and divide by the number of fixings over the window minus 1 (to allow for there being one more fixing than there are spaces between). Note the answer, and measure and mark at intervals of this width across the top of the drapes with pins, including one pin at each end.

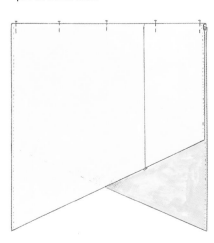

DRAPED POLES

Wrapped over a curtain pole, sheer fabric lengths make impressive improvised window drapes, especially when given a design twist – adding a contrast fabric to create a border, for example, or knotting the fabric over holdbacks to form a puffy rosette effect. There's no need for careful measuring up – simply allow twice the drop from pole to floor by the fabric width, or join widths for a generously gathered drape. Add a little extra so the fabric puddles on the floor – that way you needn't even hem it as the raw edges will be hidden in the folds.

BORDER DRAPE

Use a lightweight main fabric and a contrasting border fabric to recreate this look.

1 Arranging the drapes Drape two double lengths of fabric over the pole, tucking in the selvedges. Gather the fabric evenly across the top of the pole so the lengths almost meet at the centre. If you find the drapes slip, secure them with drawing pins for a wooden pole, or with strips of stick-and-stick touch-and-close tape (Velcro) for a metal pole. Pull back each drape and arrange in a holdback.

2 Adding the border Fold a double length of contrast fabric in half along its length, and drape it over the centre of the pole, so that the folded edge forms a neat finish down the centre of the window. Tuck in the selvedges and arrange these into the folds of the main drapes, sweeping the border back behind the holdbacks.

▶ A floral border in soft pastels adds colour and definition to a generous length of plain white muslin casually slung over the pole.

ROSETTE EFFECT

Choose a double length of fabric which looks good from both sides for this casual but elegant effect.

1 Arranging the fabric Drape the fabric over the pole so an even amount lies at the front and back; temporarily secure with masking tape. Pull the front fabric layer to one side of the window and slip it over the holdback. Knot it loosely around the front arm of the holdback, then pull out the knot to form a puffy rosette shape.

2 Completing the effect Arrange the back fabric layer in the other holdback as in step 1. Remove the tape and secure fabric as for *Border Drape*, step 1.

◀ For instant crossover drapes with puffy rosette details, hang a double length of sheer fabric over a pole, sweep it back at each side and loosely knot over holdbacks.

TIP
INSTANT HEMS
If you want to hem your improvised drapes, use double-sided fusible web strip for instant results.

CAFE CURTAINS

Café curtains are an attractive option at the windows of kitchens and bathrooms, where you want a degree of privacy and shade but don't wish to cut out too much natural light.

Café curtains screen the lower half of the window only, providing a degree of privacy but still allowing natural light to stream in over the curtain top. They're also useful for disguising a less than attractive view without totally obscuring a handsome window. Café curtains are a popular choice for kitchen, cloakroom and bathroom windows, which usually suit the style's small scale and informal feel, but there's no reason why you shouldn't use them elsewhere in your home – perhaps in a sheer fabric and teamed with full-length curtains as an alternative to traditional nets.

A café curtain is also a cost effective way of covering a window, as the amount of fabric needed is minimal. It's a good opportunity to use a cherished piece of fabric or a material that would be prohibitively expensive in the quantity needed for full-length curtains. You can make the curtain lined or unlined. Adding a lining gives some degree of insulation and extends the life of the curtain, making it more resilient to wear and tear and fading; unlined curtains have a lighter, airier feel as they let more daylight filter through.

You can hang café curtains in or outside the window recess, from a rod or pole, and give them a wide range of headings – standard or decorative heading tape, a stitched casing, tabs, ties or even punched eyelets threaded with ribbon. For a truly traditional look, shape the top of the curtain into scallops, as shown overleaf, either letting it hang flat or adding fullness with gathers or small pleats centred in each tab.

Because of their small scale, café curtains have a charming cottagey feel, which is reinforced here by a scattering of hand-painted and embroidered fruit motifs on a simple white cotton background. A tab heading allows the curtains to be drawn right back to the window sides when desired.

MAKING A LINED CAFE CURTAIN

These steps show how to make a traditional scallop-edged, lined or self-lined café curtain with a deep contrast border along the base edge. The sides of the scallops form loops at the curtain top, which you simply slide on to the pole or rod to hang the curtain in place. This curtain lies flat across the window, but you can make it wider to add fullness. Pick two coordinating prints for the curtain and border, and match the lining to the main fabric. Take 1.5cm (⅝in) seams throughout.

Before you begin, fit the pole or rod in place across the window, inside or outside the recess. Position it across the centre of a one-pane window, or following one of the cross bars on a multi-paned window to avoid a muddle of horizontal lines.

YOU WILL NEED

- ❖ CAFE CURTAIN POLE or ROD
- ❖ TAPE MEASURE
- ❖ MAIN FABRIC
- ❖ LINING FABRIC
- ❖ PAPER FOR TEMPLATE
- ❖ PAPER FOR PATTERN
- ❖ PAIR OF COMPASSES
- ❖ DRESSMAKERS' MARKER PEN
- ❖ RULER, PENCIL
- ❖ MATCHING SEWING THREAD

1 Measuring up For the finished curtain width, measure the length of the pole or rod. For the finished drop, measure from the top of the pole to the sill.

2 Calculating the scallop size Decide on the width of the scallop – usually 7.5-10cm (3-4in); and the width of the tabs – about 5cm (2in). Deduct the width of one tab from the finished curtain width, then divide the answer by the combined width of one scallop and one tab. Adjust the tab width if necessary so the scallops fit evenly across the curtain, finishing with a tab at each end.

3 Making a template On a sheet of paper, use a pair of compasses to draw a circle with a diameter of one scallop width. Cut out the circle and fold it in half. Cut along the fold and keep one semi-circle to use as a template.

4 Creating the scallop pattern Cut a sheet of paper to the finished curtain width by 20cm (8in) deep, and fold it in half widthways. On the top edge of the paper, measure and mark one tab width in from the unfolded end. Position the scallop template next to this mark, matching the top edges, and draw around it. Continue marking tabs and scallops in this way to the folded end of the paper; you should finish with a half-scallop or a half-tab at the fold. Cut out the scallop shapes and open out the pattern.

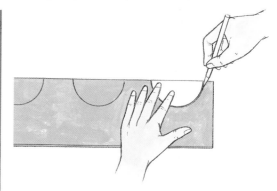

5 Cutting main fabric Cut main fabric to the finished curtain width plus 3cm (1¼in), by the drop minus 17cm (6¾in) to allow for the border. Mark a line across the curtain's wrong side, 6.5-9cm (2½-3½in) down from the top edge, depending on the desired tab depth. Pin the pattern in place 1.5cm (⅝in) in from the fabric side edges and with the top edge along the marked line. Mark round the scallops. Using a ruler and dressmakers' pen, extend the scallop edges straight up to the fabric top edge. Remove pattern and cut out the scallops.

◢ *A vegetable-print fabric is an apt choice for a kitchen café curtain. This scallop-edged curtain hangs flat across the window, so the dancing motifs are shown off to full effect. A check border creates a lively contrast.*

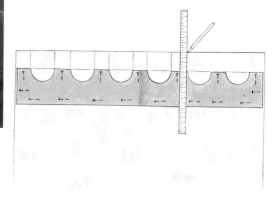

◀ *Sheer café curtains are a pretty alternative to full-length nets. To make the curtain shown here, shape and cut out a piece of sheer fabric as shown opposite, but make the tabs long enough to wrap around the curtain pole; hem the base edge, bind the other edges, and fold the tabs to the curtain front, securing them with self-cover buttons to form loops. Make the curtain a little wider than the window for a fuller, floaty effect.*

TIP
UNLINED ALTERNATIVE
If you want to make an unlined, scallop-edged café curtain, follow the steps for a lined one but add a shallow facing along the top edge rather than a full lining, and hem the side and base edges. Alternatively, you can simply bind the raw edges with bias binding as on the curtain shown left – a good option for sheer curtains on which a facing would show through.

6 Cutting the other fabrics Use the main curtain as a pattern to cut a piece of lining fabric to the same size. Cut a piece of border fabric 43cm (17in) deep by the width of the curtain plus 3cm (1¼in).

7 Marking up the loops Measure the pole or rod circumference, halve it and add a little extra for ease. Mark this amount plus a 1.5cm (⅝in) seam allowance down from the top edge of each tab on the wrong side of the main fabric.

8 Making up the curtain With right sides together and edges matching, pin and stitch the main fabric and lining together down the sides, across the tops of the tabs and around the scallops between the marked points. Trim and snip into the curved edges for ease, and neaten the raw edges of the tab loops – but don't stitch them together. Turn the curtain right side out and press. Press in the neatened edges on the tab loops, and catch them to the fabric with small slipstitches if necessary. Tack along the base edge of the curtain to hold the fabric layers together.

9 Adding the border With right sides together, fold the border strip in half lengthways. Pin and stitch the short ends, trim and turn right side out. Match one raw edge of the border strip to the base edge on the right side of the curtain. Pin and stitch in place. Open out the border, tuck in the raw edge at the back and slipstitch it to the lining, or topstitch it in place through all layers. Slide the curtain on to the pole.

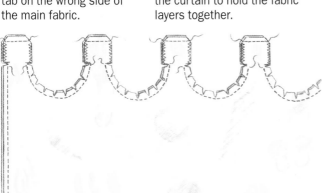

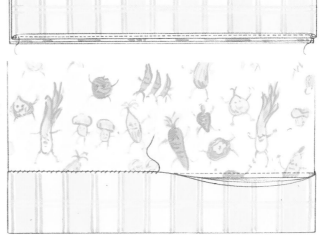

Artless and unaffected, café curtains are one window dressing which you can adapt in any way you please to suit your own individual decorating style. Experiment with different fabrics, trims, headings and hanging methods until you find just the look you're after.

▶ *Simple café curtains are a natural choice for an elegant sash window – they give privacy and soften the overall effect, but don't obscure the window's attractive lines. This sheer curtain has a stitched casing along the top edge and is ruched on to a slim rod for a straightforward, uncomplicated look. Bottles of herb and spice vinegars and oils create a colourful display across the window frame.*

▼ *A hemmed rectangle of gauzy peach-coloured voile is suspended across the window on a length of palest green sheer ribbon, threaded through eyelets punched across the fabric's top hem and wrapped around the pole. This is an ideal option for reluctant needleworkers, as it involves a minimum of sewing.*

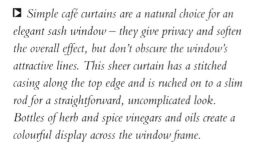

▲ *This lightweight curtain is hung from its brass pole with matching curtain rings stitched directly to the fabric edge. The style is breezy and carefree, yet well thought out. Positioning the pole higher up the window gives added privacy – the pole is aligned with one of the horizontal glazing bars.*

TIE-ON CURTAINS

Fabric ties are one of the simplest hand-made curtain headings to use on curtain rods or poles. You can make them for almost every style of curtain to add a decorative flourish.

Fabric ties are traditionally used as a flamboyant alternative to tab headings on café curtains. Made in a smart fabric, they are equally suitable for more formal sill or floor-length drapes. Like tab-headed curtains, the tie-on variety requires less fabric than those with a gathered heading, making them a little less expensive. You can cut the curtain width to one and a half times the length of the pole for soft drapes or twice the length of the pole to create deeper folds.

The concept is very simple – stitch pairs of ties at regular intervals along the top edge of the curtain and then knot each pair together, or tie them in a bow, around the curtain pole or rod. The ties must suit the size, style and weight of your curtains. You can make them long and narrow or short and wide, provided that they are long enough to tie securely around the pole or rod without being too tight. If the curtain fabric is particularly heavy, or you wish to space the ties further apart, make the ties wider so that they are strong enough to support the curtains. You may also want a little extra length so that the ties hang down in front of the curtain.

Use a fabric for the ties that coordinates with the curtain fabric. For a novel approach you could create a rainbow of differently coloured ties, picking out shades from the curtain fabric. Alternatively, stitch a bold contrast border round the curtain and match the ties to the border.

Pea green gingham, cut on the bias, is used to create heading ties and a coordinating border for these checked curtains. The gingham is repeated in other bedroom soft furnishings, providing a bright colour link.

BORDERED TIE-ON CURTAINS

Follow these steps to make tie-on curtains with a 5cm (2in) wide contrast border all round. As tie-on curtains hang below the curtain fixture, you need to position the rod or pole at least 5cm (2in) above the top of the window to ensure that the drapes block out both light and draughts effectively.

These instructions show how to make curtains with narrow ties spaced about 13-15cm (5¼-6in) apart. Space wider ties about 18-20cm (7-8in) apart. Experiment to find the best tie size by tying strips of scrap fabric in various widths and lengths around the pole.

> **YOU WILL NEED**
>
> ❖ CURTAIN POLE
>   OR ROD
> ❖ TAPE MEASURE
> ❖ CURTAIN FABRIC
> ❖ BORDER FABRIC
> ❖ FABRIC FOR TIES
> ❖ PINS
> ❖ MATCHING SEWING
>   THREAD

1 Cutting out the curtain fabric For the curtain width, measure the length of the curtain pole and multiply it by one and a half or two depending on the fullness you require. For the length, measure from the curtain pole to the desired drop, adding about 30cm (12in) if you want the curtains to puddle on the floor. Allowing 1.5cm (⅝in) for seams and matching up the fabric design, cut and join fabric widths to make a rectangle to these measurements.

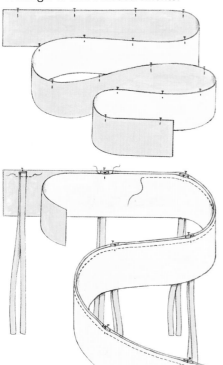

2 Cutting border strips Cut the following from border fabric, joining widths if necessary and matching any pattern:
Two side border strips measuring the length of the curtain fabric by 13cm (5¼in) wide.
One bottom border strip measuring the width of the curtain fabric plus 4cm (1½in) for turning in, by 13cm (5¼in) wide.
One top border strip measuring the width of the curtain fabric plus 4cm (1½in) for turning under, by 26cm (10½in) wide.

3 Marking the tie positions Cut the top border in half lengthways to form a front and back border strip. Measure and pin 2cm (¾in) in from either end of the front strip. Decide on the number of ties, equally spaced 13-15cm (5¼-6in) apart, between the two outer pins. With pins, mark the positions of the ties along the upper edge of the strip. Count the pins to find how many pairs of ties you need, including the outer pins.

4 Making the ties For each pair of ties cut two strips of fabric measuring 4cm (1½in) by 30cm (12in). With right sides together fold each strip in half lengthways. Stitch a 1cm (⅜in) seam along the long raw edge and one short edge. Trim the seam to 6mm (¼in), turn the tie right side out and press. Place the ties in pairs and, matching the raw edges, tack them together across the raw edges.

5 Stitching the ties Matching the raw edges, pin and tack one pair of ties to the right side of the front strip at each pin. With right sides together pin the back strip of the top border over the front, sandwiching the ties in-between. Stitch the front and back together along the upper edge, taking a 1.5cm (⅝in) seam.

6 Pressing the borders With wrong sides together press each border in half lengthways. Then press under 1.5cm (⅝in) along the back long edge of each border.

7 Adding the side borders With right sides together, position the long raw edge of the side borders 3.5cm (1⅜in) in from the side edges of the curtain. Stitch in place 1.5cm (⅝in) in from border's raw edge.

8 Slipstitching the side borders Fold the borders to the wrong side to encase the raw side edges of the curtain. Taking care that the stitches don't show on the right side, slipstitch the pressed edge of the borders to the wrong side of the curtain.

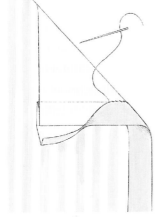

▲ *Fine fabric ties make a delicate heading for these soft voile drapes. Tied loosely in place, the curtains hang a little below the elegant cast iron curtain pole showing it off to best effect.*

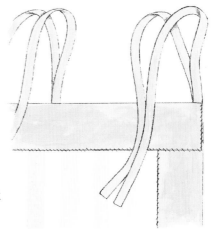

9 Stitching the bottom and top borders

Centre the bottom and top borders along the lower and upper curtain edges, respectively, and stitch them in place following steps 7 and 8; before slipstitching the backs, turn in 2cm (¾in) at either end to neaten.

LINED TIE-ON CURTAINS

You can make lined curtains with fabric ties provided you stitch enough ties along the upper edge to support the weight of the curtain.

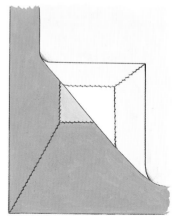

1 Cutting the fabric Measure the length and width of the main fabric following step 1, *Bordered Tie-on Curtains*. Add 14cm (5½in) to the length for the heading and hem. Cut and join fabric widths to make a rectangle this size. Cut out and stitch the lining fabric to make up a rectangle 5cm (2in) narrower and 14cm (5½in) shorter than the main fabric.

2 Pinning the lining Use pins to mark the centre of the upper and lower edge on the main and lining fabrics. With right sides together and upper edges even, pin the lining and main fabric together along the side edges.

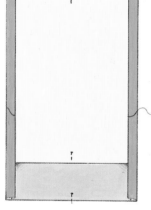

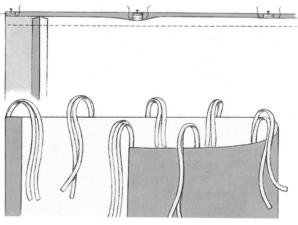

▲ *Lining these tie-on curtains gives the fabric depth and substance so it has a fuller and more luxurious feel. Using a contrast colour for the ties gives the subtle suggestion of a separate valance heading.*

3 Stitching the lining Stitch the side edges together, stopping 18cm (7½in) from the lower edge. Turn the curtain right side out and press it so that the central pin marks line up and the main fabric forms a 2.5cm (1in) border at each wrong side edge.

4 Marking the tie positions Turn the curtain wrong side out. Using pins, mark the upper edge of the main fabric into equal sections about 15cm (6in) wide. Also insert a pin at both pressed side edges.

5 Stitching the ties Count the pins to find how many pairs of ties you need. Make the ties following step 4, *Bordered Tie-on Curtains*. Matching the raw edges, pin and tack one pair of ties at each pin mark so they are sandwiched between the main and lining fabrics. Pin and stitch the upper edges of the main and lining fabrics together. Turn the curtain right side out.

6 Stitching the hem Turn under and press a 5cm (2in) hem followed by a 7.5cm (3in) hem along the lower edge of the main fabric. Handstitch the hem, mitring the corners neatly. Turn up, press and machine stitch a 2.5cm (1in) double hem on the lining. Slipstitch the unsewn edges of the lining to the main fabric.

BUTTONED TAB HEADINGS

Fabric-covered, novelty or sparkling brass buttons make eyecatching details stitched on to the tabs of a tab-headed curtain, and please the eye with their rhythmic spacing.

Buttoned tab-headed curtains are a decorative variation on plain tab-headed curtains. With the buttoned version, one end of each tab is stitched in place in the top seam of the curtain, and the remaining end is folded over to the front of the curtain where it's held in place with a button. The buttons can serve a purely decorative role, or they can be stitched to the main curtain only and passed through buttonholes in the tabs to actually button the tabs in place.

You can use almost any type of button to decorate the curtain. Fabric-covered buttons are a popular choice – they can be covered with the curtain fabric or a contrasting one to make them stand out. Brass buttons give a smart, military finish. Chic, natural alternatives are wooden or bone buttons, or use novelty, shaped buttons for a witty, informal treatment.

For the best effect, make sure that the button is large enough to stand out well against the curtain fabric – remember that it is seen from a distance. As a rough guide, the button should be about half the width of the finished tab. For the tab, you can use self or a contrasting fabric. If your fabric has a border you may be able to use this for the tabs, or use a single colour band from a stripe. For an interesting variation, you can shape the tabs into points.

A neat effect is achieved by making the tab the same width as the stripe. Bright blue buttons stand out well, covered in the same stripy fabric used to cover the shelving on either side of the window.

Making a Buttoned Tab Heading

These instructions are for unlined, buttoned tab-headed curtains, with an optional fringe along the front and bottom edges.

To work out how much fabric to buy, see pages 19–20 and allow extra for making the tabs (see steps 3-4 below). Take 1.5cm (⅝in) seam allowances throughout. Interface light fabrics to give them body.

To work out how much fabric to buy, see pages 19–20 and allow extra for making the tabs (see steps 3-4 below).

1 Cutting out the fabric Work out the length and width of each curtain. To the width add 8cm (3in) for side hems, plus 3cm (1¼in) for each join when joining fabric widths. To the length add 10cm (4in) for the base hem and a 1.5cm (⅝in) seam allowance along the top edge. Cut out each curtain to these measurements.

3 Cutting and spacing the tabs Decide on the finished tab width – usually 5-7.5cm (2-3in); double it and add 3cm (1¼in). For the length, measure around the curtain pole and add 12cm (4¾in) for the seam, overlap and ease. Cut strips of fabric to these measurements. To work out how many tabs you need, measure and mark the tabs' positions across the top of each curtain, beginning and ending with a tab and allowing about twice a tab width for the spaces in-between.

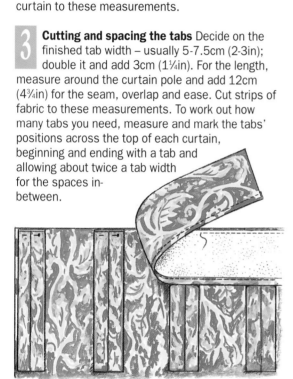

2 Preparing the curtain Join fabric widths if necessary and turn under 2cm (¾in) double hems on each side edge. Turn up a 5cm (2in) double hem on the base edge, neatly mitring the corners. Machine stitch the hems in place.

4 Making the tabs Right sides together, fold tab in half lengthways. Stitch long edge, centre seam, then stitch one short end. Turn to right side and press.

5 Preparing the facing For the facing, cut a strip of fabric 11cm (4¼in) deep and as wide as the curtain plus 2cm (¾in) for neatening the side edges. Cut a strip of interfacing to the same size and apply it to the wrong side of the facing strip. Turn up and stitch a 1.5cm (⅝in) hem along the bottom edge of the strip.

▶ *Threaded on to a painted wooden pole and embellished with fringing and a decorative, buttoned tab heading, these curtains strike a perfect balance between the formal and informal style.*

6 Attaching the tabs Matching raw edges, pin the tabs in place on the right side of the curtain. Right sides together, pin the facing strip over the tabs, matching the unhemmed edge with the raw edge of the curtain. Tack, then stitch across the curtain top, taking a 1.5cm (⅝in) seam allowance. Trim the seam and press the facing to the wrong side of the curtain. Turn in 1cm (⅜in) of the facing at each side and slipstitch to the curtain's side hem.

7 Finishing the curtain Fold the tab strips to the right side of the curtain, so that the ends overlap the curtain's top edge by 3cm (1¼in). Pin them to the curtain, making sure the ends are level. Check that the curtain pole fits through the tabs. Stitch a button on to each tab, 1.5cm (⅝in) up from each short edge, stitching through the tab and the curtain. Pin and stitch the fringing, if you are using it, to the front and lower edges of the curtain.

▶ *Look out for shaped buttons to match your fabric, like these star-shaped ones. You could adapt this theme to suit an adult's bedroom by stitching metallic star-shaped buttons on to a rich midnight blue fabric.*

Making a Pointed Tab

1 Stitching the point
Make up as in steps 3-4 opposite, but don't stitch across ends or turn them right side out; allow an extra 5cm (2in) on the length for a deeper overlap. Measure and mark the centre point of the tab, 1cm (⅜in) up from the raw edge. Measure and mark 5cm (2in) up from the raw edge on each side edge. Starting at one side edge, stitch in a straight line to the centre point. Pivot the fabric and stitch to the other side.

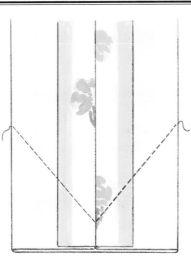

2 Finishing off Trim fabric to 6mm (¼in) from the stitch line and cut away a 'V' of fabric at the point. Turn the tab right side out and press it. Attach the tabs as for steps 5-7 opposite. *Note:* For tabs with a buttonhole, make up the tabs as instructed but position the seam to one edge to avoid stitching the buttonhole through the seam.

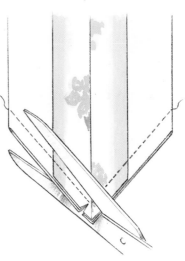

BUTTON VARIATIONS

Use interesting buttons as the inspiration for your buttoned tab-headed curtains. There is a wealth of different styles of buttons available, each offering a unique look.

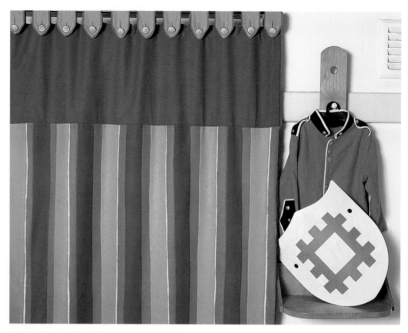

▶ *Felt is used to make the tabs on these military inspired curtains – complete with the appropriate shiny, metallic buttons.*

◀ *Using a contrasting fabric to make the tab heading is a good way of livening up a curtain or blind. The striped edge trim and tabs with plain white buttons give the Roman blind at this kitchen window a neat, modern image.*

◢ *A wooden curtain pole and bone or wooden toggles are an unexpected yet effective choice for a natural look tab-headed drape.*

Easy Lined Curtains

Sewing the lining directly into a curtain gives good results easily, and the lining adds body to the fabric so that the curtains hang well.

M aking simple lined curtains couldn't be easier: you simply machine stitch together the curtain fabric and the lining down the side hems and sew your choice of heading tape across the top to hold them in place.

Curtains with sewn-in linings are just as easy to make as unlined curtains, and you have all the benefits of the lining – the curtains will hang better, they will have good insulating properties, and the curtain fabric will be protected from the damaging effects of sunlight.

Both long and short curtains made from medium or lightweight fabric can be lined in this way, but the method isn't suitable for very heavy curtains.

Attractive curtains make all the difference to a room. Lining them helps to give a professional finish.

MAKING THE CURTAINS

When you come to choose the lining, you may want to consider a thermal lining for a very cold, exposed window, or a blackout lining if there's a need to cut out all light, but ordinary lining fabric serves most practical purposes. You can choose a neutral or coloured lining fabric or, for a pretty finishing touch that also looks good from the outside, consider lining the curtain with a complementary curtain fabric. If you drape the curtains back off the window the lining will be shown to good effect both indoors and out.

Remember when making curtains in this way that the lining can't be detached for washing. The curtains either have to be drycleaned, or you can choose washable fabric and lining of a similar weight and with the same laundering needs. This allows the curtains to be washed without danger of the fabrics shrinking at different rates.

▶ *Using the simple sew-in method, a pair of lined curtains can be run up in an evening.*

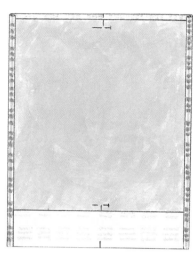

YOU WILL NEED

❖ CURTAIN FABRIC

❖ LINING FABRIC

❖ MATCHING SEWING THREAD

❖ HEADING TAPE – allow for each fabric width plus 4cm (1½in) extra per curtain

❖ CURTAIN HOOKS suitable for the heading tape

▶ See pages 19–20 for measuring up and calculating fabric amounts. Buy the same amount of lining and curtain fabric; for plain linings, deduct the allowance for pattern repeats.

1 Cutting out Cut curtain fabric to the required size and stitch widths together as necessary. Cut out and stitch the lining to make a panel 5cm (2in) narrower and 14cm (5⅝in) shorter than the curtain. Mark the centre of top and lower edges on both fabric and lining.

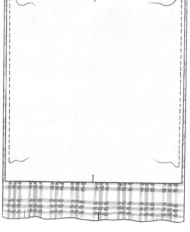

2 Stitching the sides Place curtain and lining right sides together, with side edges matching and lining 1.5cm (⅝in) down from the top edge. Pin, tack and machine stitch the sides, taking 1.5cm (⅝in) seams and stopping 18cm (7½in) from lower curtain edges.

3 Pressing the sides Turn curtain right sides out. Match and pin centre marks – the curtain fabric will wrap to the wrong side to form a 2.5cm (1in) border on each long edge. Press edges so the seam allowances sit to the centre.

4 Neatening the top edge Press the 1.5cm (⅝in) top hem allowance on fabric to wrong side over lining. Position heading tape on the wrong side, 3mm (⅛in) down from the top edge. The tape will extend 2cm (¾in) beyond the curtain on each side and cover the raw edge of the top hem. Pin in place at right angles to the tape, leaving the last 5cm (2in) free at either end.

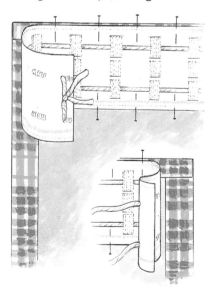

5 Attaching the heading tape At the leading edge of the curtain (where the curtains meet), pull out the ends of the cords from the wrong side of the tape and knot firmly. On the outer edge pull out the cords from the right side. Fold under each tape end so that it sits just inside the neatened curtain edge. Pin in place. Machine stitch along the tape stitch lines and across each end, keeping the ends of the cords out of the way.

TIP

CORD TIDY

Keep the cords neat and out of the way with a plastic cord tidy, sold with other curtain accessories in the soft furnishing section of department stores.

6 **Pleating the curtain** Pull the loose cords until the curtain is the correct width. Knot the cords together to hold the pleats. Do not cut the cord ends; loop them away or use a cord tidy. Insert the right number of hooks to tally with the track runners and the fixed eye at the outer edge of the track.

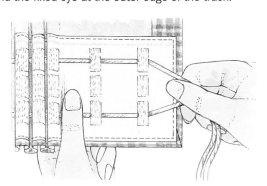

7 **Hemming the curtains** Turn up a 5cm (2in) then a 7.5cm (3in) hem on the curtains and press. Turn up a double 2.5cm (1in) hem on the lining and press. For a neat finish mitre the corners: fold the hem at an angle until the top edge touches the raw side edges. Hang the curtains at the window to check the length. Hand stitch hems. Slip stitch across the mitred edges and down the loose edges of the lining.

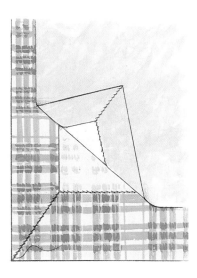

DECORATIVE LININGS

A handsomely draped coloured lining fabric, or a lining made from a complementary furnishing fabric, looks good from both inside the room and outside.

▶ A rich mixture of fabrics in this room includes curtains lined with a furnishing fabric which is also used in a different colourway for a cushion.

◀ The furnishing fabric used for lining these curtains has also been used to good effect for the cushion and the seat pad.

▲ Lining the curtains in a fabric that echoes one of the tones in the main curtain fabric adds elegance.

DORMER ROD CURTAINS

A small window set in a recess is tricky to dress without cutting out precious natural light. The ideal solution is a curtain with a casing slipped on to a dormer rod, which is designed to swing away from the window.

S mall dormer or recessed windows can be difficult to dress with curtains. The deep reveals surrounding the window often mean that it is impossible to fit a conventional curtain track. It's also tricky to find a style of curtain that you can draw right away from the window – an important factor when dressing a dormer or recessed window, where the walls block the light.

Dormer rods, designed to swing open so that the curtains lie flat against the reveals, are an ideal solution to this problem, as they suit the quaint, cottage look of this type of window. Depending on the size of the window and the effect you want, you can fit a single dormer rod that swings open from one end only, or a double one, fixed to each side of the window, that opens out from the centre. You can buy dormer rods from most department and curtain stores.

The easiest curtain to make for a dormer rod is one with a casing along the top edge. The curtain is cut fuller than the rod and simply slips on to it. As the inside of the curtain is visible when it is opened out against the walls, you need to either line the curtain, or use a fabric that looks good from both sides. You also need to choose light to mediumweight fabrics that won't put too much strain on the rod.

Simple curtains on dormer rods soften the lines of this recessed window. Line the curtains with coordinating fabric for an interesting change of scene when the curtains are open.

MAKING A CASED CURTAIN

These instructions are for making a single, lined curtain mounted on a rod that extends all the way across the window. The curtain is made to the full length of the window recess, including a stand-up frill above the casing. For a curtain without a frill, measure the length from the top of the dormer rod to the sill and use the upper edge of the curtain as the top of the casing.

▶ *A dormer rod curtain swings open against the recess wall, letting the daylight flood in.*

1 Fitting the dormer rod Measure the width of the window recess, and subtract 2cm (¾in) to allow space for the fittings. Cut the dormer rod to this measurement. Fix the rod in place at one top corner of the window following the manufacturer's instructions.

2 Measuring up Measure the curtain length (**A**) from the top of the window recess to the windowsill, adding 5cm (2in) for seams. For the curtain width measure the length of the rod (**B**) and multiply it by two. Cut and join fabric widths to make up two rectangles this size, one in the main fabric and one in the lining fabric.

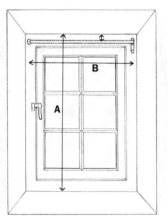

3 Stitching the edges Place the two rectangles right sides together and pin all round. Machine stitch a 2.5cm (1in) seam all round, leaving a 10cm (4in) gap at the top of both side edges, or a larger opening for bulky fabrics.

4 Turning the curtain through Clip the seam allowance at the corners and turn the curtain right side out. Taking care to line up the fold lines with the seams, press the raw edges of the openings to the inside. Tack the openings closed.

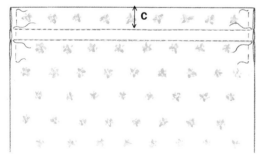

5 Making the casing Measure the space between the top of the recess and the rod (**C**) and use tailors' chalk to mark a line across the top of the curtain, the distance **C** down from the upper edge. Draw a second line 2cm (¾in) below the first one. Machine stitch along the marked lines, stitching both lines in the same direction.

TIP

CUP HOOK SUPPORTS
A brocade or velvet curtain fabric would normally be considered too heavy for a dormer rod. However, you can use weighty fabrics like these if you fix an inconspicuous cup hook to the recess wall and window frame, to support the free end of the rod when it's swung open and closed.

6 Completing the curtain Slipstitch the pressed edges closed above and below the two rows of stitching. Remove the tacking. Slide the curtain on to the dormer rod. Screw in the end stop to hold the curtain in place. Spread out the fabric along the rod so that the gathers are evenly spaced.

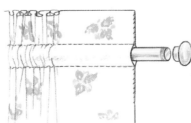

VALANCED CURTAINS

If you have a decorative curtain pole or rod to display, make curtains with a built-in valance which hangs below the pole, rather than from a track or pelmet shelf fixed over it.

A softly gathered valance adds a neat finish to plain curtains and gives them a dressier finish. The newest valance styles are stitched into the top of the curtain and hang with it from a pole. They look just as stylish but slightly less formal than a traditional valance. An unexpected bonus is that the valance highlights rather than covers up the curtain pole – good news if you want to make a feature out of a carefully chosen decorative pole.

The simplest way to make a valanced curtain is to add extra length to the top of the curtain and fold this forwards then back to form the valance. This valance has a soft, modern look that sits well in a contemporary home.

Another option is to cut the valance as a separate piece of fabric and stitch it to the top of the curtain, together with the heading tape. This way you can achieve a more formal look using pinch pleat, goblet pleat or smocked heading tape. You can use a contrasting fabric for the valance if you wish. This method is more economical than the fold-over one, as it uses only one layer of fabric for the valance.

You can use any medium or lightweight fabric for both the valanced curtain styles. Take your pick from bold modern prints, patterned, filmy sheers, vivid shot silks and crisp contemporary stripes – all current favourites.

A handsome curtain pole is highlighted by any kind of detail at the top edge of the curtain. Here the eye is drawn upwards to the attractive stitched-in valance and scroll-end wrought iron pole, creating an impression of height.

FOLD-OVER VALANCE

These instructions are for lined curtains with a valance formed by folding the top edge of the curtain forwards then back again by the required valance depth. Before you begin, decide exactly how long you would like the valance to be – one-sixth of the curtain drop is the usual proportion. You can make the valance less than one-sixth, particularly if your curtains are full-length, but the finished valance length should not be less than 20cm (8in), otherwise the impact is lost.

FABRIC REQUIREMENTS

The curtain and valance are made from a single length of fabric, so to find out how much you require you need first to calculate the total length of the curtain, including the valance depth and hem allowances (see step 1). Multiply this length by the number of fabric widths required, adding extra for any pattern repeat. Buy this amount of fabric.

1 Measuring up Fix the pole above the window and slip on the rings. For the finished curtain drop, measure from the eye of one curtain ring to the floor (**A**), or required length. To the drop add 12.5cm (5in) for the lower hem allowance, 5cm (2in) for the top turning allowance and twice the finished depth of the valance. This is the total length required. Measure the finished width of the curtain(s) (**B**), multiply by 1½-3 depending on the heading tape, and calculate the number of fabric widths you need.

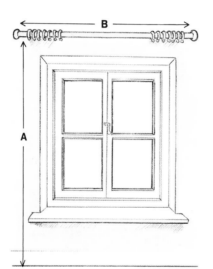

2 Cutting out Cut the main fabric to the measurements in step 1, joining widths if necessary, and press the seams open. For each curtain, cut out and stitch the lining fabric to make a panel the length of the curtain drop (**A**) and 5cm (2in) narrower than the main curtain fabric panel. Using tailors' chalk or a pin, mark the centre of the top and lower edges on both fabric and lining.

3 Stitching the lining Place the main curtain and lining fabric right sides together with side edges matching and the bottom edge of the lining 12.5cm (5in) up from the base edge of the curtain. Pin, tack and stitch the sides, stopping 18cm (7½in) up from the base edge of the main fabric. Turn right side out. Line up and pin centre marks and press the curtain edges so the seams face the centre. Press 1.5cm (⅝in) to the wrong side on the unstitched side edges of the main fabric.

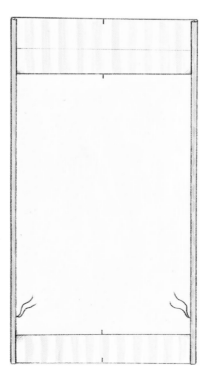

4 Marking the valance Check that the top raw edge of the lining is a straight line. If it isn't draw a line in tailors' chalk just above it on the wrong side of the main fabric. Measure up from this line, or from the edge of the lining, the depth of the valance and mark this with a tailors' chalk line on the wrong side of the main fabric.

5 Forming the valance Wrong sides together, fold the main fabric along the second marked line and press. Open out the fabric and measure up from the fold line the depth of the valance. Fold and press along this line, then open out the fold. To form the valance, refold the fabric at the first fold, and line up the second fold line with the top edge of the lining so the excess main fabric lies over the lining.

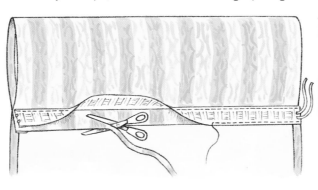

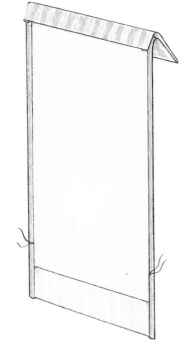

◪ *By using a decorative coordinating fabric to line the curtain and extending this on to the fold-over valance section, you can create a pretty contrast frill.*

◧ *Full-length gold curtains, topped with a fold-over valance and gently parted, herald the way to the dining table. Deep fringing along the edge of both curtain and valance has a graceful and softening effect.*

6 **Stitching in the heading tape** Turn in the raw end of the tape and free the cords in the usual way. Lay the tape on the wrong side of the curtain, with its top edge lined up with the fold line at the top edge of the lining. Pin and stitch the top edge of the tape through all layers. If the raw edge of the valance shows beneath the lower edge of the tape, trim off the excess so that it is covered by the tape, then stitch the remaining tape edges.

7 **Hemming the curtains** Turn up a 5cm (2in) then a 7.5cm (3in) hem on the main fabric curtains and press. Turn up a double 2.5cm (1in) hem on the linings and press. Hang the curtains to check the length and stitch the hems.

8 **Finishing off** Slipstitch the side edges of the valance together to neaten. To dress the curtains, either fold the valance to the front of the curtain just above the heading tape and press before pulling up the heading tape – this gives a neat, crisp fold at the top; or pull up the heading tape before flopping the valance forward, giving a softer, more casual look. Insert the hooks and hang in the usual way.

Stitched-in Valance

These instructions are for an unlined curtain with a stitched-in valance cut out separately. Decide how long you want the valance to be; it should be about one-sixth the length of the curtain drop. The heading tape will take up some of the depth, so make sure that there is enough valance depth remaining to make a substantial frill.

You can use any heading tape for this style of valance – but remember when you are choosing the tape that the curtain heading is on show. For a really smart finish, use goblet or triple-pleat heading tape, and edge the valance with a trim, such as fringing or braid. If you want to give the valance more body you can line it, but it works perfectly well unlined.

You Will Need

❖ Curtain Pole
❖ Tape Measure
❖ Furnishing Fabric
❖ Matching Sewing Thread
❖ Valance Trimming (optional)
❖ Heading Tape
❖ Tailors' Chalk
❖ Pins
❖ Curtain Hooks

1 Measuring up Fix the curtain pole in position above the window and slip on the curtain rings. For the finished curtain drop, measure from the eye of one curtain ring to the floor, or required length. To this length add 15cm (6in) for the bottom hem allowance. Measure the finished curtain width required and multiply this by 1½-3 depending on the heading tape you are using. Calculate the number of fabric widths you need. For the valance depth, decide on the required finished depth and add 10cm (4in) for the hem and top turning. The valance width is the same as the curtain width.

2 Cutting out Cut the fabric to the measurements in step 1. For the valance, cut fabric strips to make up a strip the required width and depth, cutting the valance to match the repeat at the top of the curtain if necessary. Join the fabric widths, and the valance strips, and press the seams open.

3 Hemming On the side edges of the curtain and valance strip, stitch a double 2.5cm (1in) hem. On the lower edge of the curtain, machine or slipstitch a double 7.5cm (3in) hem. To hem the valance, press under 1cm (½in) and then 4cm (1½in) and machine or slipstitch in place; add any trimming to the lower edge of the valance at this stage, if required.

A triple-pleat heading tape gives these stitched-in valance curtains a smart, crisp finish. Opt for this or a goblet heading tape for a more formal style.

4 Joining the valance and curtain Lay out the valance wrong side up, and place the curtain, wrong side up, on top, with the raw edge of the curtain 5cm (2in) down from the top edge of the valance. Turn the valance raw edge 5cm (2in) down over the raw edge of the curtain, press, and pin through all thicknesses, folding the ends of the turning in at an angle away from the outer edges of the curtain.

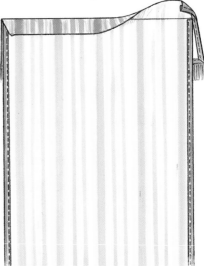

5 Adding the heading tape Prepare the ends of the tape in the usual way and lay the tape along the top of the curtain with the top of the tape just below the fold. Pin and stitch the top edge through all thicknesses. Trim away any excess valance which shows below the edges of the tape, and stitch round the remaining edges of the tape.

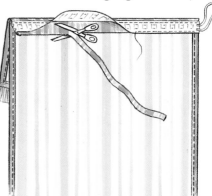

6 Hanging the curtain Pull up the tape in the normal way, put in the hooks and hang the curtain. You can either fluff out the folds of the valance so that it stands out separately from the curtain, or dress the folds of the valance in with the curtain for a smoother effect.

LACE CURTAINS AND VALANCE

Lace curtains are popular in a variety of guises. One refreshing way to use lace at the window is relatively unadorned – with a simple gathered valance skimming the top edge.

For rooms that aren't closely overlooked, a pretty lace curtain used without drapes looks wonderful and lets in plenty of light. Crown the lace with a softly gathered valance hung from a decorative pole – the valance covers the lace heading to give a tidy finish, as well as adding interest and impact to the overall effect.

There are many options with this look. You can make the lace curtain sill-length and team it with a valance in a checked fabric or a folksy mini-print to suit a country kitchen. Or, you can opt for an elegant, floor-length sweep of lace, topped with a valance in a rich damask or velvet. For a romantic bedroom, top a frilled and scalloped lace curtain with a lacy valance – you can buy valance lace in many designs and with shaped and frilled edges. Layering lace over lace creates intriguing effects as the light filters through overlapping patterns.

Whichever style you choose, the lace curtain is suspended from an elasticated wire or a slim net rod fitted inside the window recess, and the valance from a curtain pole fixed over the window. Your eye is drawn upwards to look at the valance, so choose an attractive pole to enhance the final effect.

A sill-length lace curtain enhances the light and airy feel of this dining area. The wooden curtain pole, ivory valance and table accessories add natural warmth.

MAKING A LACE CURTAIN

The instructions that follow are for a fixed lace curtain with a cased heading, hung from either an elasticated wire or a slim net rod. You can buy lengths of elasticated wire packaged together with the screw-in hooks and eyes that you need to fix them. Net rods are available to fit most windows, even bay windows, and are easy to put up on wooden, metal or PVC frames.

YOU WILL NEED

- ❖ NET CURTAIN LACE
- ❖ TAPE MEASURE
- ❖ SCISSORS AND PINS
- ❖ MATCHING SEWING THREAD
- ❖ ELASTICATED WIRE KIT OR NET ROD KIT to hang the lace
- ❖ PLIERS (if you are using elasticated wire)

The way you make the curtain depends on whether you're using long or short nets. *For long nets:* stitch a casing along the top and hem the base edge. *For short nets:* hem the sides, and stitch a casing if necessary.

Hanging with elasticated wire Hold the wire in place against the window frame and stretch it slightly to gauge the correct length. Cut it to fit with the pliers. Screw a hook into each end of the wire. Thread the wire through the casing in the lace curtain. Screw the matching screw eyes into the top of the window frame or into the soffit (top of the recess), one on each side. Hook an end of the wire into each screw eye.

Hanging with a net rod Fix the brackets in place on the window frame or recess with screws, or sticky pads for PVC. Thread the rod through the casing and clip it in place.

MAKING A STRAIGHT-EDGED VALANCE

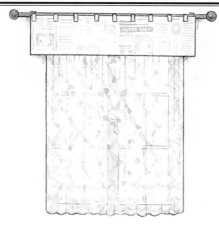

The instructions that follow are for a lined valance, made from any curtain-weight fabric and gathered with a heading tape.

1 **Choosing the valance depth** Fix the pole in place over the window. Measure the window width and add 10-15cm (4-6in) on either side. Cut a piece of paper this width by the depth of the valance – usually one-sixth of the length of the main curtain. Tape the paper centrally to the pole to check the effect. Adjust the depth if necessary.

2 **Cutting out** Work out how long the ungathered valance strip needs to be – 1½-3 times longer than the pattern, depending on the heading tape and the fullness required. Cut and join furnishing fabric widths to make a strip this long by the depth of the finished valance plus 6cm (2¼in). For the lining, cut and join widths to make a piece the same length, but 4.5cm (1⅞in) shallower than the main fabric. Press the seams open.

3 **Making up the valance** With the right sides together, pin one long raw edge of the lining to the lower raw edge of the main fabric. Stitch and press the seam open. With right sides together still, refold the fabric so that the unstitched lining edge lies 1.5cm (⅝in) below the top raw edge of the main fabric. Pin the side edges together and stitch them. Trim the seams and turn the valance through to the right side. Press the valance.

YOU WILL NEED

- ❖ FURNISHING FABRIC
- ❖ LINING FABRIC
- ❖ PATTERN PAPER
- ❖ STICKY TAPE
- ❖ CURTAIN POLE
- ❖ TAPE MEASURE
- ❖ SCISSORS AND PINS
- ❖ MATCHING SEWING THREAD
- ❖ HEADING TAPE
- ❖ CURTAIN HOOKS
- ❖ CURTAIN RINGS

4 **Positioning the tape** Press 1.5cm (⅝in) at the top edge of the main fabric to the wrong side over the lining. Position the heading tape over it, 3mm (⅛in) down from the top edge, so it covers the raw edge of the main fabric and extends 2cm (¾in) beyond the curtain on each side. Pin it in place.

5 **Stitching the tape** Tuck under the tape ends and machine stitch the tape in position, keeping the pull-cords clear of the stitching. Knot the cords at one end of the valance and pull them at the other end to gather up the valance. Even out the gathers, insert curtain hooks through the tape and hang the valance in place.

Consider the different elements of your lace curtain and valance combination before making your choice. Notice how length, edgings, colour and pattern all contribute to the final look.

▶ *If you would like a lacy window treatment that's colourful too, consider painting your window frame and architrave in a vivid colour – the paintwork shows through the lace curtain quite clearly. Then you can add a bright fabric valance to set the treatment off strongly. Here a green gingham valance provides a suitable note of country-style contrast.*

◀ *This lace curtain has a trompe l'oeil valance woven into the design – a great boon if you haven't got time to stitch up a separate valance. A deep frilled and scalloped edging adds interest and luxurious weightiness to the curtain and, because it is low down, doesn't cut out precious light or conceal the view beyond.*

▶ *You can create a romantic look for a bedroom with a full-length lace curtain and matching lace valance. To make the valance, simply stitch a length of translucent heading tape along the the upper, straight edge of a length of valance lace and pull it up to fit the pole. You can buy valance lace in various depths and with lots of exquisite edgings.*

Lace curtains

Making a set of lace curtains is one of the easiest home furnishing tasks.

Lace is a decorative fabric made up of motifs worked on a mesh background. Most furnishing lace is sold for making curtains and comes in a variety of widths and drops for this purpose – choosing the right type for your window means you can usually make curtains from a single width of lace fabric. However, if you do need to use more than one width, simply thread unjoined widths on to the hanging device, rather than seaming them together.

You can buy lace fabric either in a suitable width – *long nets* – or with a suitable drop – *short nets* – and there are special length nets for valances and café curtains. Most lace fabric is either 100% polyester or a cotton and polyester mix. **Long nets** are sold in widths from 150-300cm (60-118in) wide, so that you can make most curtains from one piece of fabric. The selvedges of the fabric form the side edges of the curtain.

Short nets are ideal for windows that are wide rather than tall. They're designed so that the two edges of the fabric become the top and bottom of the curtain. The lower edge is pre-finished, with a hem or a shaped edge or frill. The other edge often has a ready-made casing to take an elastic wire or a hanging rod. They're sold in lengths from 100-228cm (40-90in).

Valance lace is sold in valance-length drops, with a shaped or frilled edge. You can buy it by the metre or yard.

Café curtain lace is sold in drop lengths of 30-80cm (12–31½in). The lower edge is usually shaped or frilled and the top edge finished with either a casing or eyelets, for threading on to a slim rod.

Hanging lace curtains

Lace curtains are generally very lightweight, so the method of hanging does not have to be nearly as sturdy and strong as for standard curtains. Nor, in most cases, do they need to be drawn back and forth as they are usually positioned permanently across the window.

Elasticated wire (1) with a small hook at each end is a cost-effective and popular way of hanging permanently positioned lace curtains. You simply thread the wire through a casing at the top of the curtain and hook the ends to screw eyes at either side of the window. Elasticated wire is suitable for small, lightweight curtains, but tends to sag with wide or heavier curtains.

Lace curtain rods are slim rods which are slipped inside a casing at the top of the lace curtain. They provide firm support, so the curtains won't sag. The rods are usually plastic and adjustable to the size of the window, and are either telescopic or fixed with brackets. For bay windows you can buy rods that are bendable as well as extendible. Slim *café rods* (2) for hanging lace café curtains are available in plastic, wood or brass, in fixed or adjustable lengths.

Lightweight lace curtain tracks (3) are used if you wish to draw the curtains back and forth across the window.

Translucent heading tapes (4) are available for hanging lace curtains. There are two types – one with bars on the back for threading on to an elasticated wire or rod and one which can be hung from a curtain track or pole by means of lightweight, clear or white plastic curtain hooks.

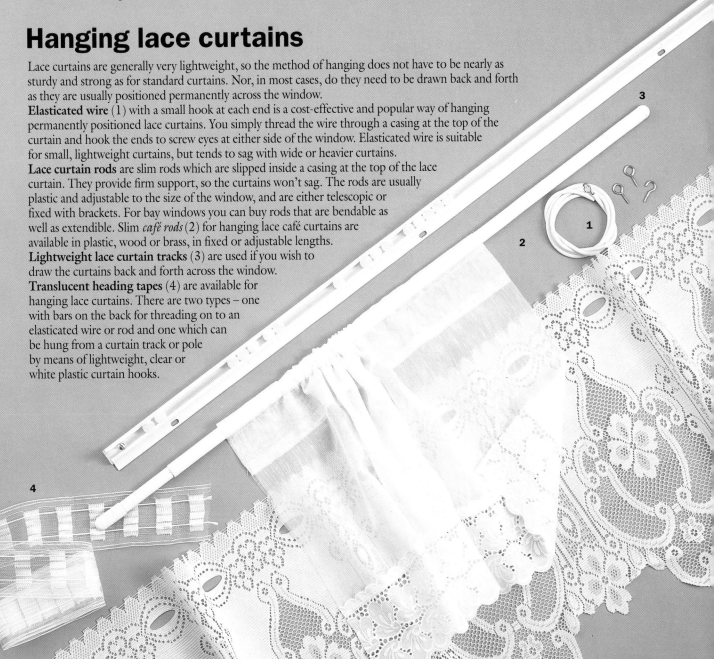

Measuring up for lace curtains

When you are measuring up for lace curtains, a point to bear in mind is the type of lace you are using. Heavily figured lace should be used much more sparingly than muslin or voile, which needs to be quite full for privacy and so that it doesn't look skimpy.

Long nets Measure the width and length of the window area to be covered. Multiply the width by 1½-3, depending on the amount of fullness required, and buy a fabric this wide, if possible. If your window is very wide, work out how many widths you need. To calculate the length of lace fabric to buy, add 20cm (8in) for the hem and casing, plus an additional 30cm (12in) for shrinkage, on to the window

length. Buy this amount of fabric if you only need one width. If you need to use two or more widths of lace, multiply the length required by the number of widths.

Short nets Measure the width and length of the window area to be covered. Buy a lace fabric which has a drop equal to the length of the window. To find out how much fabric you require, multiply the width by 1½-3, depending on how much fullness you would like.

Valances and café curtains Measure up for the drop length you need. Multiply the width of the window by 1½-3, depending on how much fullness you would like.

Stitching lace curtains

Use a size 9 (70) machine needle to stitch delicate lace, and a size 11 (80) for heavily textured lace. Use a medium stitch length and practise stitching on a scrap of lace to achieve the right tension. If hand sewing lace, use a size 7 or 8 Between needle.

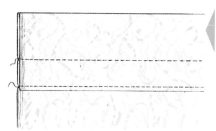

Hems

Most *long nets* are finished at the side edges, so you only need to hem the lower edge. On *short nets*, you only need to hem the sides.

Side hems Turn under a double 1.2cm (½in) hem down each side edge of the lace curtain. Pin and stitch the hem close to the inner folded edge.

Base hems Turn a double 4cm (1½in) hem along the base edge of the lace curtain. Pin and stitch the hem close to the inner folded edge. Turn up an additional temporary hem if the fabric has not been preshrunk.

Making a casing

This cased heading is suitable for hanging a curtain on an elasticated wire or slim curtain rod up to 1cm (½in) in diameter. If your curtain rod is fatter, stitch a deeper casing to accommodate it. Allow 12cm (4¾in) of fabric for this heading.

On the upper edge of the curtain, turn a 6cm (2¼in) double hem to the wrong side and press. Tack. Stitch along the hem, close to the folded base edge and again 2.5cm (1in) higher up. Remove the tacking and press. Slip the wire or rod through the lower casing. The top part of the casing forms a small stand-up frill.

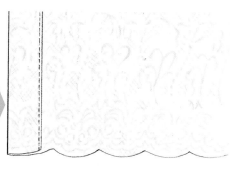

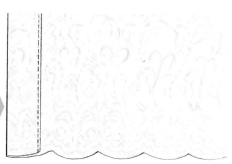

Seams

For curtain-making purposes you shouldn't need to seam lace fabric, but if you are making other items, cushion covers for example, from lace you do need to. Stitch seams as for sheer fabrics with either a French seam, zigzagged seam or two rows of straight stitch close together.

TIP

SHRINKAGE

Most lace fabrics shrink when you first wash them and may shrink again during subsequent washes, so buy an extra 20cm (8in) per width and turn up a deep temporary hem which you can unpick after washing to adjust the length.

SHEER CURTAIN PANELS

The airy effect of sunlight filtering through gauzy curtains can positively lift the spirits. Capture this mood with a window dressing created by setting sheer fabric panels into complementary borders.

Lace curtains and sheer fabrics are usually chosen as window dressings because of their useful screening properties – they offer a good degree of privacy and help mask unattractive views without restricting too much natural daylight. But they can be much more than simply a practical choice – their delicate patterns and light-enhancing textures are attributes just waiting to be developed in a more imaginative and creative way.

One of the most interesting ways to highlight these attractive characteristics is by designing a window treatment where the sheers are given equal importance with another fabric, rather than playing the more usual supporting role. Panel designs offer this opportunity, as by framing sheer fabric panels with complementary borders made from closely woven lightweight fabrics, such as cotton and chintz, you can create a dramatic fabric design with a beautiful textural balance.

A practical advantage of this approach is its versatility, as you can create panel designs to fit and flatter most window sizes.

An open window and a light breeze show these informal gingham-edged curtains with their lacy inset panels to advantage. You can make this style of curtain quite simply by piecing the panels and borders together like patchwork, adding the long side borders last.

TIED BORDERED PANELS

Panel designs look particularly attractive edged with distinctive borders which are neatly finished with mitred corners. The panels shown here have double mitred borders which create a frame on both the front and back – ideal for sheer curtain panels, and for panels used as informal room dividers, where the front and back views are of equal importance.

You can make the borders in a colour to match the sheer panel, or create a distinctive effect with patterned or contrasting plain fabric borders. Alternatively, take stained glass on window panes as your design inspiration, and combine neutral borders with sheer panels in subtly toning shades.

A decorative way to hold square or rectangular panels together is with a series of ties inserted into the outer seams of the borders. You can make the ties from matching fabric, or use ribbons for a quick and easy finish. Use a double layer of matching ties to hang the panels from a decorative curtain pole.

MEASURING UP

1 Planning a design Measure the window. Draw a scale diagram of the window on pattern paper. Decide whether the mitred panels are to hang inside or outside the reveal, and mark the overall finished size of the hanging in place on the window drawing. Taking your window shape as a guide, decide on the most suitable panel shape – squares or rectangles – and divide up the finished hanging size to see how many panels you require and their finished size.

2 Estimating border sizes Estimate a suitable border depth for the panels – this should be in proportion to the central sheer part of the panels for a balanced effect; use the picture opposite as a guide. Use a ruler, set square and pencil to draw a square/rectangle to the finished panel size decided on in step 1. Mark a border within this shape, adjusting the depth as necessary until you find the best balance. Keep this pattern guide for reference for the following steps.

3 Making paper patterns To make the *sheer panel pattern*, draw a square/rectangle to the size of the area within the border, then add 1cm (⅜in) all round for seam allowances. Cut out the pattern. Make the *border patterns* as necessary, following your chosen mitred corner method (see page 63).

TIP
CUSTOMIZED PANELS
When planning a panel design for a window treatment, take the window's proportions as a starting point, and make up the mitred panels to echo the shape of the window panes and their layout within the frame.

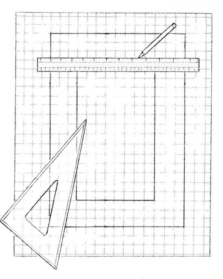

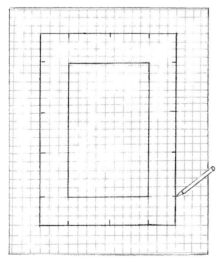

4 Estimating for ties The number of ties you require depends on the size and proportion of the panels. For square panels allow for the same number of ties on each side. For rectangular panels allow for more ties on the long sides than on the short. Remember to allow for a double line of ties on the top edge of each top panel, to tie to the curtain pole. The corner ties are placed 5cm (2in) from each corner, with the other ties spaced evenly between. Mark the tie positions on the pattern guide created in step 2, and keep for reference.

5 Cutting out the ties For each tie required, cut a 20cm (8in) length of the narrow ribbon, or a 21cm (8¼in) strip of your border fabric, to twice the desired finished width of the tie plus 1.2cm (½in) for seam allowances.

▲ *White on white is a subtle combination that always looks enchanting. Here, satin ribbon ties join a series of milky white sheer panels, each one framed with a mitred chintz border. Matching sheer fabric bows tied each end of the curtain pole add a pretty detail.*

MAKING THE PANELS

1 **Cutting out the sheer panels** Use the panel pattern to cut out the sheer fabric panels, following the straight grain and centring any pattern detail. Use a dressmakers' pencil and a ruler to transfer the seam allowance to the wrong side of each panel.

2 **Adding the first set of borders** Following your chosen method, cut out the border pieces and transfer the seam and mitre measurements to the wrong sides. Join one set of borders to the panel and press the seams open.

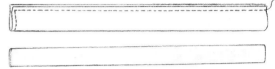

3 **Making fabric ties (optional)** With right sides together and raw edges level, fold each fabric tie strip in half lengthways. Taking a 6mm (¼in) seam, sew across one short end and down the length. Turn out and press.

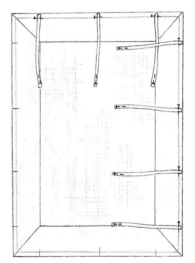

4 **Inserting the ties** Follow your pattern guide to mark the tie positions on the right side of each border. With raw edges level, pin a tie to each position and stitch across to secure; remember to attach two ties at the top edges of the top panels. Pin the ties towards the sheer panel to avoid catching them in the following stitching stages.

5 **Completing each panel** Following the appropriate method, make up and join the back border to the front border, stitching through all fabric thicknesses. Turn out, remove the pins from the ties and press the panel. Slipstitch the back border in place.

6 **Assembling the panels** Lay out the panels on a flat surface and, starting at the centre of each one, knot the ties together into neat bows. Continue to assemble the panels. To hang, tie the panels to the curtain pole, starting at each outer edge.

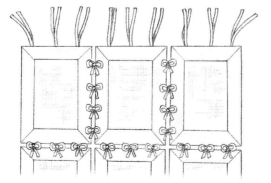

HANDKERCHIEF PANELS

Create beautiful sheer panel designs in an instant using lace-edged handkerchiefs or other gauzy fabrics such as antique embroidered table mats and cloths. Alternatively, you can achieve a similar effect with fine cotton or linen squares, trimmed with crochet edgings or strip lace. To hang the panels, stitch a fabric casing to the back to hold a slim curtain rod, or use decorative net curtain clips or rings to hang them from a pretty pole.

YOU WILL NEED

- ❖ LACE-TRIMMED EMBROIDERED HANDKERCHIEFS all the same size
- ❖ SPRAY STARCH
- ❖ MATCHING SEWING THREAD
- ❖ MATCHING PLAIN FABRIC STRIP
- ❖ CURTAIN POLE or ROD
- ❖ IRON

1 Preparing handkerchiefs Wash, starch and iron the handkerchiefs so that they are fairly firm and look their best. Pay particular attention to the lacy edgings, restoring their shape neatly as you press them with the iron.

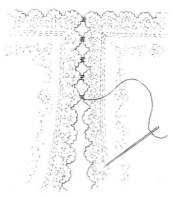

2 Joining the panels Piece together the handkerchiefs by butt joining the lacy edgings. Take a few hand stitches through the centre of each lacy scallop or other prominent detail, making sure the handkerchiefs can lie perfectly flat. Continue to add handkerchiefs to make up the required panel size.

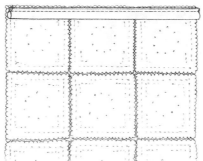

3 Making a casing Measure the circumference of your curtain pole. Add 2cm (¾in) to this for turnings and cut a fabric strip to this size by the curtain width plus 2cm (¾in). Press under the turnings, then machine or hand stitch the casing to the back of the handkerchief panels. Slip the pole through the casing.

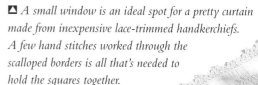

◤ A small window is an ideal spot for a pretty curtain made from inexpensive lace-trimmed handkerchiefs. A few hand stitches worked through the scalloped borders is all that's needed to hold the squares together.

Double-sided mitred border

A double-sided mitred border gives a neat edge

This is for curtains or hanging panels where both sides are on view.

Method 1 is for adding mitred borders to a square panel only; *method 2* is for adding a mitred border to a rectangular or square panel. For the best results, secure all lines of stitching at the start and finish with a few back stitches.

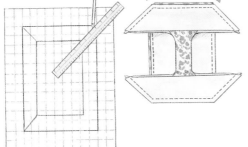

Method 1 – square panels

1 **Marking up the main fabric panel** Mark a 1cm (⅜in) seam allowance all round the edge of the main square fabric panel, on the wrong side.

2 **Attaching the first border strip** Press diagonal creases each way across the main fabric panel with an iron. Cut eight border strips on the straight grain, adding 2cm (¾in) to required border depth for seams, and extending border length by border depth at each end plus seam allowances. With right sides together, stitch along the marked line to join the first strip to the panel.

3 **Marking the mitres** Open out the border strip and use a ruler and dressmakers' pencil to extend the diagonal creases across the border on wrong side.

4 **Adding the second border strip** Join the second border strip as the first, stitching up to the corner point on the main fabric panel. Open out the border, press, and mark the diagonals as before. Repeat for the other sides.

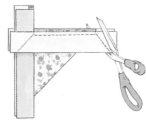

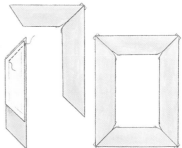

5 **Joining the mitres** Fold the panel diagonally with wrong sides together. Fold back the border strips in pairs and tack and stitch through the marked mitre lines to join strip ends. Trim excess fabric and press the seams open.

6 **Completing the first border** Press the panel and border flat. Mark a 1cm (⅜in) seam allowance on the right side of the border, all round the outer edge.

7 **Adding the second border** With right sides together and starting and ending at a mitre seam, stitch the next set of border strips in place along the outer edges, mitring the ends together by marking on the diagonals then stitching to 1cm (⅜in) from the inner raw edges. Trim the mitre seams and press them open.

8 **Finishing off** Turn the border to the panel back and press in the seam allowance. Slipstitch the inner edge in place along existing stitch line.

Method 2 – rectangular panels

1 **Making a pattern** Use a ruler, set square and pencil to draw the finished panel and border size on pattern paper. Mark the mitres by drawing lines diagonally through the border from corner to corner. Cut out the pattern pieces.

2 **Cutting out** Using the patterns, and adding 1cm (⅜in) all round for seams, cut out the panel and eight border strips, four long and four short, on the straight grain. Transfer the seam markings to the wrong side of the fabric on all pieces.

3 **Making up the borders** With right sides together, join a long and short border strip, stitching from the outer edge of each mitre to 1cm (⅜in) from the inner edge. Repeat, then join the two sections together to make one border. Press the seams open. Make up the other border in same way.

4 **Attaching the panel** Right sides together, pin the panel to a border along marked seam lines. Stitch to join, stitching each panel side to the inner mitre stitching line. Press flat, and trim the panel corners.

5 **Adding the backing border** With right sides together, pin the borders along the outer seam line. Stitch, trim corners and turn out the border to the back of the panel. Slipstitch in place, enclosing the raw edges.

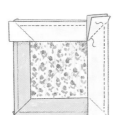

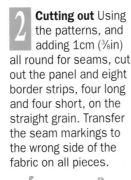

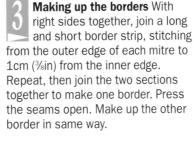

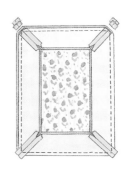

Basic stitches

Knowing how to sew a few simple stitches by hand is essential

When you're unfamiliar with a stitch, try it out on scraps of fabric first. Use a contrasting sewing thread so you can see the stitch formation clearly and remember to anchor the working thread at the start and finish of a row.

Backstitch

This strong stitch is used for stitching and repairing seams by hand, particularly on small areas where machining would be awkward. On the reverse, the stitches overlap and are twice as long as on top.

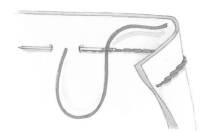

Working from right to left, secure the thread. Then take another short stitch backwards over the first, this time bringing the needle out to the front, a stitch length to the left of the first stitch. Take the needle back to the end of the previous stitch each time, to form a continuous row of neat, even stitches.

Herringbone stitch

Use this stitch to neaten or hem raw edges on medium and heavyweight fabrics or to secure interfacing.

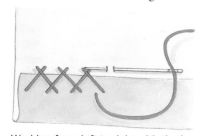

Working from left to right with the hem facing you, secure the sewing thread in the hem edge. Pick up one or two threads in the fabric above the hem, and slightly to the right, with the needle pointing from right to left. Moving the needle the same distance to the right again, take the next stitch from right to left through the hem. Continue to alternate stitches, keeping them even.

Flat hemming

This is an almost invisible hemming stitch used on light and medium-weight fabrics.

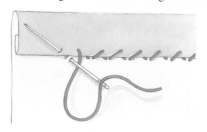

Work from right to left, with the hem facing away from you. Secure sewing thread on hem using a double stitch. Pick up one or two threads on the single fabric, insert needle diagonally through the folded hem and pull sewing thread through lightly to avoid puckering.

Hemming slipstitch

This delicate stitch is used to secure hems on lightweight and sheer fabrics.

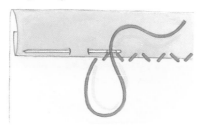

Work from right to left, with the hem facing away from you. Anchor the sewing thread on the hem. Pick up a thread of the single fabric. Then insert the needle into the hem edge, and slip along the fold. Continue stitching in an even zigzag fashion along the hem.

Slipstitch

This is used to join two folded edges together invisibly.

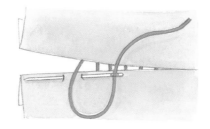

Place the two folded edges together, with right sides facing you. Anchor the thread in a fold. Take the needle across to the opposite edge and slip it 6mm (¼in) along the fold. Pull the thread to draw the edges together. Work from side to side until the opening is closed.

Overhand stitch

This holds together two finished edges and may be used for example to attach a lace trim to a hem. It is firmer than slipstitch, but not as invisible.

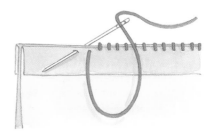

Working from right to left, insert the needle diagonally through both edges, picking up a few threads in each. Pull through firmly. Then take the needle straight back across the join.

Lockstitch

This is used in making curtains to link the fabric permanently to its lining.

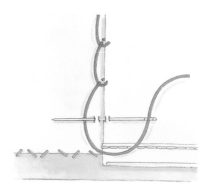

Lay the fabric and lining flat on the floor with wrong sides facing. Pin together down the centre and fold the lining back on itself along the line of pins.

Work the stitches from top to bottom. Anchor the thread on the lining. With the needle pointing from right to left at right angles to the fold, pick up one or two threads in the folded edge and then in the fabric. Leave a length of thread running down for about 10cm (4in), then pick up one or two threads in the lining and fabric again. Take the needle over the working thread, forming a loop. Continue all the way down the length of the fold, keeping the stitches slightly loose.

On large curtains, lock the lining and fabric seams together, and work further rows of lockstitching at 40cm (16in) intervals.

BISHOP SLEEVE CURTAINS

Bishop sleeve curtains add grace and a sense of formal elegance to any room. Highly adaptable, you can style them into sleek, fluid columns or sumptuous, puffed-out curves.

Although lavish in appearance, bishop sleeve curtains are straightforward to make. All you need to do is to add extra length to your curtains when you are cutting them out. To create the bishop sleeve shape, tie the curtains back tightly in one or several places and puff the extra fabric out over the tiebacks. You can, if you like, make the curtains longer still, so that they spill into graceful folds on the floor.

The type of fabric you use enormously influences the shape and fullness of puff you can create. Lightweight fabrics, such as sheers and fine silks, give a slim, fluid silhouette with the fabric hanging quite straight, then spilling out softly just above each tieback. You can pull medium and heavyweight fabrics out above the tieback to form a more pronounced shape. Padding the curtain with tissue paper exaggerates the shape.

For invisible tiebacks use any narrow cord, preferably in a colour to match the curtain fabric. Thick silky cord and tassels, ribbons or floppy fabric bows are some of your options for a more decorative look. Once it is tied and carefully sculpted, you cannot draw a bishop sleeve curtain, so you need to use it in conjunction with sheers or a blind in rooms where you require day or night-time privacy.

You can hang bishop sleeve curtains with the heading style of your choice. For an informal window treatment use a tab-heading; for formal rooms use a puffball heading, described over the page, or any heading tape.

The bishop sleeve style makes even inexpensive fabrics look lavish. Here, a generous length of unbleached calico is nipped into two tiny waists and left to cascade into deep folds at the floor. A deep swag of fabric creates a graceful heading.

These instructions are for a lined bishop sleeve curtain with a puffball heading. This style of heading is especially suited to bishop sleeves as it continues the theme of ruched and gathered fabric, giving a full, luxurious finish; it's also just as straightforward to make.

To make the puffball heading, you simply stitch a deep casing at the top of the curtain, then stitch a heading tape just below the casing. When the heading tape is drawn up, the casing ruches up as well. To create the full, puffball effect, pad out the casing with wads of tissue paper.

FABRIC QUANTITIES

Measure up as usual for an ordinary lined curtain, basing your width measurements on a pencil pleat heading. To the length add 30cm (12in) for each puff, 32cm (12½in) for the puffball heading strip and 14cm (5⅝in) for the hem and top seam allowance. If you want the curtains to puddle on the floor add a further 30cm (12in).

1 Measuring up Fix the curtain track in position over the window. Measure from the fixture to the floor, or to the desired length. Decide how many puffs you want and add 30cm (12in) to the length for each puff, 32cm (12½in) for the heading and 14cm (5⅝in) for the hem and top seam allowance. Multiply the finished width of the curtain by 2½-3 depending on how much fullness you want.

2 Cutting out Cut the curtain fabric to the measurements in step 1, joining fabric widths with plain, flat seams if required and pressing the seams open. Cut out and stitch the lining fabric to make a panel 5cm (2in) narrower and 12.5cm (5in) shorter than the curtain fabric. Using tailors' chalk, mark the centre of the top and lower edges on both main fabric and lining.

ADAPTATIONS

You can make any of the curtains featured in this book into bishop sleeve curtains. Just add 30cm (12in) for each puff to the length of the curtain when you are cutting out. Arrange the curtains following steps 9 and 10 on the facing page.

3 Stitching the lining Place the curtain and lining fabric right sides together with the top and side edges matching. Pin, tack and machine stitch the sides, taking a 1.5cm (⅝in) seam allowance and stopping 18cm (7½in) from the lower curtain edge.

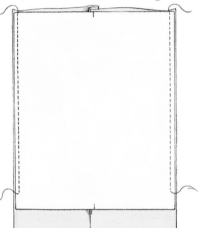

4 Pressing the sides Turn the curtain right side out. Match and pin the fabric at the centre marks – the main fabric wraps to the wrong side to form a 2.5cm (1in) border on each long edge. Press the edges so the seam allowances face the centre.

5 Stitching the casing Using tailors' chalk, mark a line on the right side of the curtain 17.5cm (6⅞in) down from the top edge. Press the top of the curtain to the wrong side along this line and tack all layers of fabric together 1.5cm (⅝in) up from the raw edge. Stitch along this line and press.

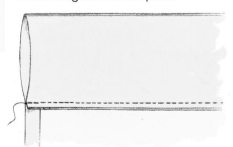

6 Stitching the heading tape Lay the top of the curtain out flat, lining side up. Place the curtain heading tape over the seam allowances aligning the top of the tape with the stitching and extending it 2cm (¾in) beyond the curtain at each end. Fold under the tape ends, leaving the gathering cords free at one end. Pin and stitch the tape in place. Draw up the cords until the curtain is the required width and even out the gathers.

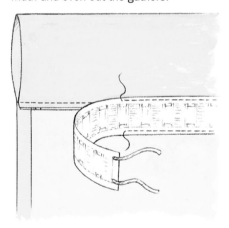

7 Padding out the heading Open out the fabric heading tube and run a gathering thread around each end. Stuff tissue paper into the heading, scrunching it to achieve a soft, puffy look, and allowing the heading to fall forward over the front of the curtain. Pull up and secure the gathering threads to close the heading.

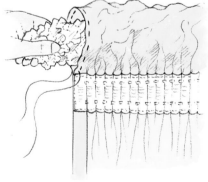

8 **Hemming the curtain** Turn up a 5cm (2in) then a 7.5cm (3in) hem on the curtain and press. Turn up a double 2.5cm (1in) hem on the lining and press. For a neat finish mitre the corners, folding the hem at an angle until the top edge touches the raw side edges. Hand stitch the hems. Slipstitch across the mitred edges and down the loose edges of the lining.

9 **Creating the bishop sleeves** Hang the curtain from the track. Determine the positioning of the tiebacks by bunching the curtain tightly with your hands and lifting it to various heights until you find the proportions pleasing. Mark this position on the wall or window frame with a pencil and fix a cup hook at the mark.

Bishop sleeves are a good choice of curtain style for a bay window, especially when they are used in conjunction with blinds. You can hang a curtain on either side of the window and over the main uprights of the window frame. Stitching the heading sections together avoids untidy gaps along the curtain track.

10 **Styling the bishop sleeves** Tie cord tightly around the curtain, level with each cup hook, and loop it over the hooks. Arrange the fabric into puffs, filling them with tissue paper if you want a fuller effect. When hanging bishop sleeve curtains on either side of a window, keep checking that the puffing at each hanging point is symmetrical.

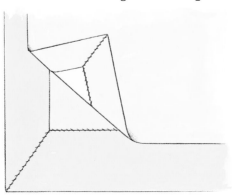

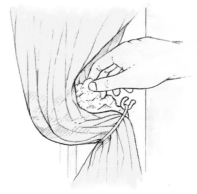

Accentuate the graceful lines of bishop sleeve curtains by securing their folds with decorative ribbon in a coordinating shade, or twisted cord hung with silken or natural jute tassels.

▲ Pinched into bishop sleeves with ribbons tied in neat bows, an inexpensive, lightweight muslin curtain looks most elegant hanging at a French window.

◥ Using a jute tassel to trim a muslin curtain shaped into soft puffs adds a rustic touch to a simple yet stylish window treatment.

▶ For a truly sumptuous effect, a crisp acetate fabric curtain in rich orange is pulled out into bouffant bishop sleeves and tied up with gold cord and tassels.

ITALIAN STRUNG CURTAINS

Let in the light with elegant Italian strung curtains –
they are lifted away from the window by cords that are threaded
through rings stitched at the back.

I talian strung or reefed curtains are ideal for windows where you want full-length elegance yet wish to let in as much light as possible too. Their graceful shape also makes them perfect for framing a pretty view.

This style of curtain is a cross between tied-back curtains and festoon blinds. The fixed heading is stitched closed at the centre and the drapes are permanently drawn back and upward by means of cords

threaded through rings sewn to the lining. If you need greater privacy, mount a simple roller blind behind the curtains.

The formal look of Italian strung curtains works best with a defined, dressy heading like pencil, goblet or cartridge pleats. Avoid using a plain gathered heading, as the pleating conflicts with the folds of the drapes. Most fabrics, except sheers, are suitable, and the curtains must be lined in order to hang gracefully.

The heading is the focal point of Italian strung curtains, as the draped curtains draw the eye upwards. A valance or pelmet is unnecessary because it would only interrupt the flowing lines of the drapes.

Plan your curtains so that when they are pulled back, the lower part of each curtain will overlap the window by no more than 7.5cm (3in). This allows a generous curve for the drape and still lets in plenty of light.

You will need a standard curtain track, capable of supporting the weight of the curtain fabric. As the curtains are never drawn back, there is no need for a corded track.

When calculating the amount of curtain fabric required, allow 60cm (24in) for turning up a double 30cm (12in) hem. The extra depth is necessary because the stringing lifts the leading edges of the curtains at a sharp angle, so

that the undersides of the hems are visible in places. For the lining, allow 83cm (32¾in) less than for each curtain length, and turn up a 2.5cm (1in) double hem that overlaps the curtain hem by 2cm (¾in).

Make up standard lined curtains, using the heading tape of your choice, and work several bar tacks along each hem to anchor the lining to the curtain. Then proceed with the steps below. Being able to spread the curtains out flat makes attaching the rings easier – if you do not have a table large enough, clear an area of floor.

You could even apply this Italian stringing technique to a pair of ready made curtains.

YOU WILL NEED
❖ STANDARD TRACK
❖ CURTAIN FABRIC
❖ LINING FABRIC
❖ MATCHING THREAD
❖ HEADING TAPE
❖ TAPE MEASURE
❖ STICKY TAPE
❖ NYLON BLIND CORD
❖ SIX 1.5cm (⅝in) PLASTIC CURTAIN RINGS

1 Joining the heading Using firm slipstitches, join the ungathered curtains down the centre to the depth of the heading tape.

2 Planning the curve Temporarily fasten one end of the tape measure to the centre of the track. Hold the other end out towards the side of the window to form the curve for the upper part of the curtain. Mark the lower end of the curve on the tape measure with a strip of sticky tape.

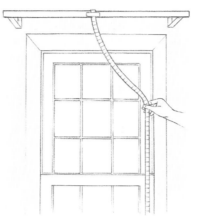

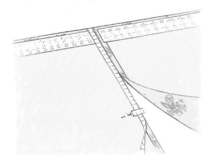

3 Marking the curve position Spread the joined curtains out smoothly, lining side up, on a flat surface. Remove the tape measure from the track and, lining the end up level with the top of each curtain in turn, lay it flat along the leading edges. Mark each curtain with a pin at the marked point on the tape.

4 Stitching on the rings On each curtain, sew the first ring at pin level, 5cm (2in) in from the leading edge, sewing through the lining into the curtain itself, being careful to catch only a few threads of fabric. Sew two more rings to each curtain, placing them about 25cm (10in) apart, in a gentle upward curve toward the outer corner.

5 Pulling up the curtains Cut two lengths of cord to match the distance between the first rings and upper corners of the curtains. Tie each cord to the first ring on either side, then thread it through the other rings. Gather the headings and hang the curtains. Pull up the blind cords to form the draped effect. Tie the free ends to the track brackets.

🔺 *Enhance the graceful shape of the curtains with a jaunty bow, stitched over the centre join in the heading.*

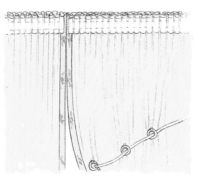

TIP

RING POSITIONING
If you are not sure where to position the rings, fasten some safety pins in the chosen positions, thread cord through them and check the effect before sewing the rings to the curtain.

SWAGS AND TAILS

Dress your windows with extravagant swags and tails – they look elaborate, but are really only a drape of fabric across the top of the window framed by separate pleated panels.

Classic swags and tails are one of the most lavish and popular curtain treatments. At first glance they look complicated, as though they are arranged from one long length of fabric. In fact this is only an illusion – they are actually made in three separate, manageable sections, which are simply stapled, or held in place with Velcro, on a narrow pelmet shelf fixed above the window.

Traditionally, swags and tails give a formal look to a room, expecially when they are teamed with full-length curtains. They can also be used on their own to frame a small window, or in conjunction with a blind or sheer curtain for a smart but less formal effect.

You can use the same fabric for the curtains and swags and tails, or opt for a complete contrast in colour or pattern. The lining will also be on show when the tails are pleated up – a contrast lining will accentuate the pleats, while repeating the main fabric as a lining gives a more understated effect.

A pair of overlapping swags, laid over short, loosely pleated tails on either side, creates a theatrical entrance to a conservatory.

DESIGNING SWAGS AND TAILS

These instructions show how to make a pattern for swags and tails by draping fabric, so that you can check the style suits your window, before cutting out the main fabric. For different effects, you can vary the number of swags, the way the tails are pleated and the arrangement of the swags and tails together. As a guide, a single swag should be about one-fifth the depth of the curtain and no wider than 102cm (40in); if your window is very wide, then it is better to make two or three smaller swags. Each tail is generally one third as long as the curtain or window length, with the shortest point slightly lower than the centre of the swag.

Alternatively, you can buy commercial paper patterns, which you will find at the back of dressmaking pattern books.

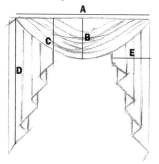

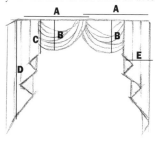

A single swag fitted under long pleated tails.

One full-width swag hanging over the tails.

Double swags with pleated tails on top.

Finished size

A = width of the swag
B = depth of the swag
C = inside length of the tail
D = outside length of the tail
E = width of the tail

☑ *One exceptionally wide swag, laid over the tails on either side, exaggerates the width of a very large window.*

PUTTING UP A PELMET SHELF

Before you can hang the swags and tails – or even start making the fabric pattern – you will have to fix a narrow pelmet shelf above the window.

YOU WILL NEED

❖ 12mm (½in) PLYWOOD

❖ HAMMER-ACTION ELECTRIC DRILL with MASONRY BIT

❖ WALLPLUGS

❖ 38mm (1½in) ANGLE BRACKETS

❖ WOODSCREWS and SCREWDRIVER

1 Cutting the wood Cut a length of 10cm (4in) wide plywood so that it extends 5-7.5cm (2-3in) beyond the curtain track at each end – or have it cut to size at the home improvement store or lumber yard.

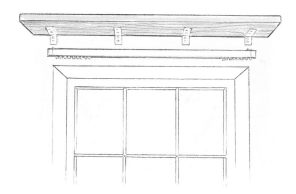

2 Fixing the shelf Mark the position of shelf centrally 5-7.5cm (2-3in) above the curtain track. With a masonry bit, drill holes in the wall for fixing the angle brackets at each end of the shelf and at 30cm (12in) intervals in-between. Fit wallplugs and attach brackets with 32mm (1¼in) woodscrews. Rest the shelf on top and fix in place with 10mm (⅜in) woodscrews, screwing upwards. Mark the centre of the shelf.

MAKING PATTERNS

Use an old sheet, or soft fabric like muslin, to make the test patterns. The tails are shaped on the pelmet shelf, and the test swag is checked up there too, so you need a ladder, lots of pins and sticky tape to hold the fabric while you judge the effect.

These instructions show how to make a single swag with five folds, teamed with triple pleated tails that sit on top of the swag (see first diagram on previous page). However, it is easy to adapt the instructions to change the number of folds in the swag and pleats in the tails.

1 Measuring up Hang a tape measure, 10cm (4in) in from each end of the pelmet shelf, to the desired depth of the swag. Measure width of the swag (**A**) and depth at the centre (**B**). Measure down each side of the window to desired inner length (**C**) and outer length (**D**) of the tails. Measure the width of the tails (**E**) to cover swag edges.

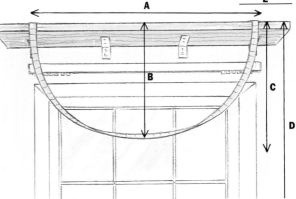

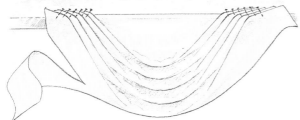

3 Folding the swag It is easiest to shape the swag when it is pinned on a low surface like an ironing board. Pick up the test fabric at the first mark on the guideline, lift it up and pin along the top edge, 12.5cm (5in) inside the line. Alternating from side to side, continue pinning marked folds, moving 2.5cm (1in) outwards to the corner each time.

2 Marking up the swag On the test fabric, draw a rectangle the width of the swag (**A**) plus 40cm (16in), by 1½ times the depth of the swag (**B**), plus 5cm (2in) for overlapping on top of the shelf. Then mark 20cm (8in) in from each side on top long edge. Draw a diagonal line from each mark to the corresponding corner on the lower edge. Divide and mark each diagonal evenly into one more space than the number of folds planned – for five folds, mark six equal spaces.

4 Checking the draped effect Adjust the folds until they hang symmetrically in soft sweeping drapes. When you are happy with the effect, trim away excess fabric from both ends and along the curved lower edge, 7.5cm (3in) from the last fold. Then unpin it from the ironing board and tape it centrally on the pelmet shelf.

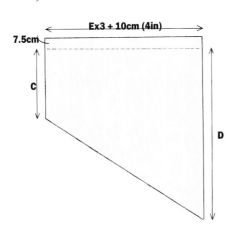

5 Drawing up a tail Using the measurements taken at the window in Step 1, draw up on the test fabric a rectangle 3 times the finished width of the tail (**E**), plus the depth of the pelmet shelf (10cm/4in), by the longest length of the tail (**D**) + 7.5cm (3in) for fixing to shelf. Down one side, mark the shortest length of the tail (**C**) + 7.5cm (3in). Draw a diagonal line from the bottom of **C** to the opposite bottom corner, and cut out the test pattern.

6 Pleating the tails Using sticky tape or tacks, position the top 7.5cm (3in) of the tail on the shelf, wrapping it round the side as well. Pleat as you wish to the desired width (**E**), pinning folds in place on top of the shelf. Stand back to check the effect and adjust if necessary. Take down the patterns.

MAKING THE SWAG

Unpin the folds in the fabric pattern piece, then fold it in half lengthways to check the pattern is even; adjust as necessary. For softer, more natural folds, cut out the swag on the bias. Use the pattern piece to work out how much fabric and lining you will need. Remember to add a 1.5cm (⅝in) seam allowance to the pattern piece.

1 Cutting out fabric and lining Cut out the swag so that the centre is on the bias grain of the fabric. Find the bias by folding the cut edge to align with the selvedge and marking this fold with pins. Fold the test swag in half lengthways and press the fold line. Line up folds on the test swag and fabric, pin in position and cut out.

2 Making up With right sides together, pin, tack and stitch the lining to the main fabric along the curved bottom edge. Trim the seam allowance, turn right side out and press. Then pin, tack and stitch the remaining three sides neatly together.

swag pattern

bias grain

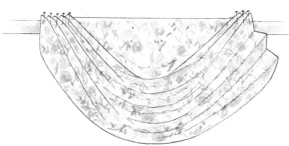

3 Folding Pin the upper edge of the fabric to the top of an ironing board. Pleat up the ends of the swag at each notch, pinning the folds to check the effect.

MAKING THE TAILS

Open the pattern piece out flat, with the position of the pelmet shelf return marked, to add a dart for a neat, boxed corner. (If the swags and tails fit into a window recess, no pelmet return is needed.) Remember you are making two tails, so buy double the amount of fabric and lining needed for the test pattern.

1 Cutting out the tails Cut out one tail in fabric and lining, adding a 1.5cm (⅝in) seam allowance all round. Then flip the test tail over and cut out the second pieces of fabric and lining, as the mirror image of the first.

◀ *In close up, the details of the tail pleats show clearly – here they sit slightly on top of each other, with a rosette to emphasize the corner.*

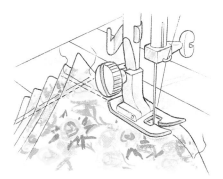

On a small window, a modest swags and tails arrangement looks quite charming. Note how the pink lining fabric highlights the folds in the tails.

4 **Stitching the folds** When satisfied, unpin the swag from the ironing board. Tack, remove pins and then machine stitch across the folds to hold pleats in place.

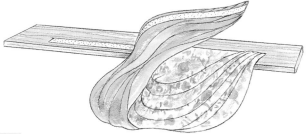

5 **Fixing up the swag** Cut a strip of Velcro to match the width of the swag. Stitch the hooked side along the top of the swag, 1.5cm (⅝in) from the edge. Fold the other side in half, align the centre with the centre mark on the pelmet shelf and stick down, 4.5cm (1¾in) from the edge.

2 **Making up the tails** For each tail, with right sides together and edges matching, stitch the lining fabric to the main fabric down both sides and along the slanted lower edge, leaving the top edge open. Trim seam allowances, clip across corners and turn right side out before pressing. Zigzag stitch upper edges together.

3 **Shaping round pelmet shelf** Fold the long side of the tail back on itself, right sides together, along the marked corner line. Make a dart by stitching through all layers of fabric from the outer corner of the shelf to the top corner of the tail, so that it will fit neatly over the edge. Repeat on the other tail.

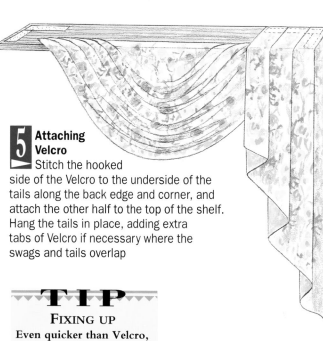

5 **Attaching Velcro** Stitch the hooked side of the Velcro to the underside of the tails along the back edge and corner, and attach the other half to the top of the shelf. Hang the tails in place, adding extra tabs of Velcro if necessary where the swags and tails overlap

TIP
FIXING UP
Even quicker than Velcro, use a staple gun to attach the swags and tails to the pelmet shelf. Alternatively, use upholstery tacks, tapped in place with a hammer.

4 **Pleating** Fold each tail into evenly spaced pleats to match the test tails, and pin and tack together across the top. Tape the tails in place on the shelf to check the fit. Take the tails down and machine across the top to hold the pleats in place. Press the folds along their length if you want a tailored effect.

Ornate swags and tails found in period homes were dressed with lavish trims. Adapt the effect for your home – you'll find that adding fringing or a contrast lining will define the sweep of the swags and tails to perfection.

▶ *Tall windows can carry off a double swags and tails treatment with good grace. Here dark fringing adds emphasis to the bright floral drapes.*

▲ *In this case, a pale, plain lining is used to make the pleats of the tails stand out distinctly against the bold, dark curtain fabric.*

◀ *On gracious windows you can really go to town on a swags and tails extravaganza, using rich contrast fringing to accentuate their folds and contours.*

WOODEN PELMETS (CORNICES)

If you want a new look for your curtain and window treatment, why not fit a pelmet? The simple, boxed design looks good in a range of decorative styles, adding impact to any room.

As a prominent part of a window treatment, a pelmet serves a multitude of decorative purposes. It's perfect for hiding a sagging curtain heading or a clumsy wooden batten used to secure the curtain track to the wall.

The wooden pelmet front also offers lots of scope for different decorative effects. You can paint or stencil it so that colours or motifs flow round the room without interruption. Or you can cover it with fabric or wallpaper to match the rest of the decorations in the room, trimming it with braid or cord to highlight its elegant outline.

You can also adjust the size and shape of a pelmet to alter the apparent proportions of the window. Fixing the pelmet higher than necessary makes the window appear taller; making the pelmet wider than necessary helps make the window seem wider.

The front panel of the pelmet is glued and pinned to a three-sided pelmet box fixed securely to a batten above the window. You can make a plain, rectangular pelmet front from plywood but for a more decorative effect, you can cut out a fancy profile along the lower edge or buy one ready-cut and shaped in fibreboard.

A modest pelmet with a gently curving edge, painted to match the walls rather than the curtains, gives the window a streamlined finish that's ideal for this soft modern living room.

MAKING A PELMET BOX

YOU WILL NEED

- ❖ TAPE MEASURE
- ❖ PLYWOOD 9mm (⅜ in)
- ❖ PENCIL
- ❖ FINE-TOOTHED PANEL SAW
- ❖ SANDPAPER
- ❖ ELECTRIC DRILL AND BITS
- ❖ CHIPBOARD SCREWS 19mm (¾ in)
- ❖ TRY/L SQUARE
- ❖ WOODWORKING ADHESIVE
- ❖ LEVEL
- ❖ PLYWOOD 3mm (⅛ in)
- ❖ SOFTWOOD BATTEN 50 x 25mm (2 x 1in)
- ❖ WALLPLUGS
- ❖ COUNTERSUNK WOODSCREWS 50mm (2in) No 8
- ❖ L-SHAPED BRACKETS 3.8mm (1½ in)
- ❖ BRADAWL
- ❖ CHIPBOARD SCREWS 9mm (⅜ in)
- ❖ PANEL PINS AND HAMMER

The top and sides of this pelmet box are made from sturdy plywood and the front panel from thinner plywood. Always measure up before buying your materials. To work out the width of your pelmet, decide how far you want it to extend beyond the curtain track. Allow room – 5cm (2in) on each side is usually enough – for the curtains to gather neatly when you open them.

You also need to make sure that the pelmet projects far enough into the room to clear the track and curtain heading – 10-15cm (4-6in) is generally sufficient. You can make the pelmet as long as you like, provided it covers the blind or curtain heading with clearance at the top.

1 Cutting the pelmet box pieces Mark out the pelmet top (**A** x **B**) and two sides (**B** x **C**) along one length of the 9mm (⅜in) plywood. Using a fine-toothed panel saw, cut out the pieces and then sand down any rough edges.

2 Assembling the pieces Drill screw holes in the top corners of the side pieces and then lightly secure them to the pelmet top using 19mm (¾in) chipboard screws. Use a try square to ensure that the joins are square and then remove the screws, apply wood adhesive to the join and rescrew tightly. Allow the adhesive to dry. Measure up for the pelmet front (**A** x **C**) and cut it out from the 3mm (⅛in) plywood. Check the fit and then put it to one side.

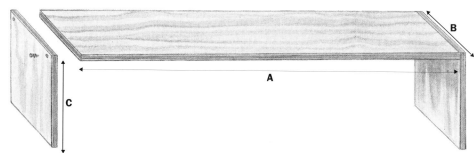

◀ *Medium density fibreboard with pre-shaped edges makes very attractive pelmets. When you are fitting a pelmet tight up against the ceiling like this, you can omit the top piece and attach the front and side pieces to battens attached to the ceiling joists.*

3 Positioning the pelmet box With the help of a friend, stand on a stepladder and hold the pelmet box up to the wall above the window. Check that it is centred on the window at the correct height and make sure that it is perfectly level. Mark a guideline on the wall along the lower edge of the top piece.

4 Preparing a wall batten Cut a length of softwood batten to fit neatly within the pelmet box. Using a No 12 wood bit, drill 4.5mm (³⁄₁₆in) clearance holes for No 8 woodscrews roughly 2.5cm (1in) in from each end of the batten. Drill more holes at regular intervals of about 25cm (10in) in-between.

5 Putting up the batten Hold the batten up to the wall so that its top edge is aligned with the pelmet guideline. Insert a bradawl through the batten's screw holes to mark the position of the drill holes in the wall. Remove the batten, drill holes in the wall and fit wallplugs. Use No 8 woodscrews to fix the batten to the wall.

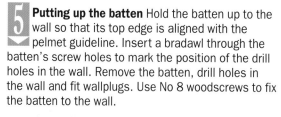

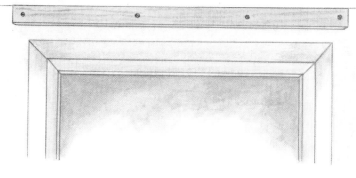

6 **Fixing the pelmet box** Ask a friend to hold the pelmet frame in place on the batten. Take the L-shaped brackets and mark the position of the screw holes on the underside of the pelmet top and the batten, at each end and about 30cm (12in) apart in-between. Use a bradawl to make starting holes at the marked points. Fix the brackets to the batten and then secure the pelmet box by screwing upwards through the brackets using 1cm (⅜in) chipboard screws.

7 **Adding the pelmet front** Finish putting up the pelmet using adhesive and panel pins to attach the front (see step 2) to the top and sides of the box. Decorate it in keeping with your chosen style.

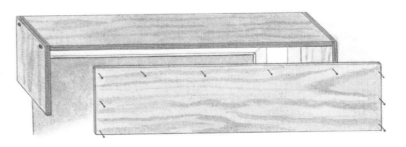

△ *An absolutely plain pelmet does a neat job of hiding the top of the curtains and the curtain track. To add variety, the lower edge may be picked out in another colour found in the curtains and the piping of the tiebacks.*

DECORATING A WOODEN PELMET

You can decorate a pelmet in a variety of ways, depending on the effect you want to create and taking into account the style and colour scheme of the room, the size of the window and the type of curtains you intend to hang.

Stain or varnish looks great if you have made your pelmet box from good quality, natural wood and wish to highlight the grain. You can add decorative detail to the front with lengths of wooden moulding.

Pelmets made from MDF must be painted or papered for an attractive finish. You can use a variety of paint finishes to good effect. First apply primer and undercoat, then sand the surface down before applying the top coat. You can either leave this plain or try a paint effect such as sponging or ragging, combined with a stencil pattern perhaps. If you want to, you can then continue the stencilled design round the walls.

Using wallpaper on your pelmet is a good way to get a more patterned effect. You can match the existing paper in the room or use a coordinating border cut to fit.

▶ *A strip of pine cornice, complete with a cutout motif to match the plate rack and units, becomes the perfect pelmet for the window in this charming cottage kitchen.*

▲ *A snazzy red pelmet, with a scalloped and droplet edge, is an equal match for the vibrant colours and patterns in the curtain fabric. Together, they make an ideal team for livening up a child's bedroom.*

◀ *This narrow pelmet conceals the top of the roller blind very neatly. Shaping just the ends of the pelmet front quietly echoes the shaped edge of the blind.*

FABRIC PELMETS

Give your windows a distinctive and professional finish with fabric pelmets which add style to your curtain headings and are both simple and cost effective to make at home.

F abric pelmets are horizontal bands of stiffened fabric secured to a special shelf above a window. They serve two functions. The first is decorative: a beautifully shaped and finished pelmet enhances the look of windows. The second function is practical – the pelmet conceals the curtain track and heading and can alter the proportions of the window. If fixed higher than the window, a pelmet can make the window appear taller; if extended at the sides, it can make the window look wider.

The pelmet design you choose will depend on the style and shape of the windows, the type of room you have, and on the kind of fabric you have chosen for the curtains. Pelmets can be completely plain – the simplest is rectangular – or they can be shaped in any pretty or decorated fashion you choose. Often the curtain fabric will dictate the shape of the pelmet edge: striped, checked or geometric curtain fabrics suggest straight, regular shaping like zigzags or castellations, while floral curtains work well with curves or scallops. Sometimes the design on the fabric gives you an attractive shape to follow.

Most furnishing fabrics, except very open weaves and sheers, are suitable for making the pelmet. Use the same fabric as the curtain, or choose a contrasting pattern – perhaps in a colour to complement the other furnishings in the room. With patterned fabrics, remember to allow enough fabric to centre the design on the pelmet.

A pelmet tops off a window dressing handsomely. Here the contrast between a straight checked pelmet and the draped patterned curtains creates a neat modern look.

MAKING A PELMET

Traditionally pelmets have been backed with buckram, a heavy, woven interfacing. Look for it in fabric, drapery and upholstery shops as well as in the soft furnishing departments of large stores.

When using fabrics with very noticeable directional patterns on wide windows, it may be necessary to join fabric widths – do this before cutting out the shape. Use a full fabric width at the centre and position the narrower panels to each side. Press the seams open.

Avoid joining buckram, if using it, as the joins will form ridges and reduce the strength of the pelmet.

◩ *A deep pelmet over floor length curtains beautifully accentuates the height of this window.*

◩ *The fabric covering a pelmet often suggests the shaping for the edge. Plains and stripes call for geometric designs like these.*

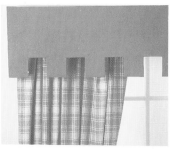

YOU WILL NEED
❖ PAPER FOR TEMPLATE
❖ BUCKRAM or SELF-ADHESIVE STIFFENER
❖ FABRIC and LINING
❖ BUMP INTERLINING or IRON-ON INTERFACING to interline buckram
❖ TAPE MEASURE
❖ SCISSORS
❖ PINS, SHARP NEEDLE, THREAD and THIMBLE
❖ IRON and IRONING BOARD
❖ DECORATIVE BRAID and FABRIC ADHESIVE
❖ VELCRO or CURTAIN RINGS and SCREWS

MAKING A PELMET SHELF

When positioning the shelf, remember that the top edge of the pelmet is fixed to the shelf and forms the upper boundary of the window area. Take into account the height and depth of the pelmet in relation to the window and to the height of the ceiling, bearing in mind that the pelmet must cover the track.

If your pelmet is very wide or deep, you will need to add rectangular end pieces to the shelf for rigidity. For example, if the shelf is 10cm (4in) deep, nail a 10cm (4in) square piece of plywood at right angles to each end of the shelf.

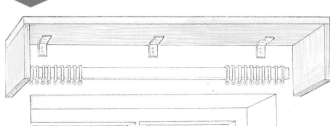

HANGING THE PELMET

For ease of cleaning, hang a removable pelmet by sticking the hooked half of a Velcro strip along the edge of the pelmet shelf and attaching the other half of the Velcro to the wrong side of the pelmet. Or sew curtain rings to the back of the pelmet at regular intervals, and hook them over screws fixed to the shelf.

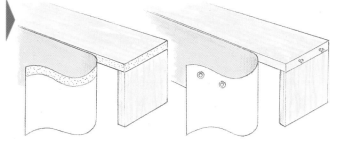

USING BUCKRAM

Buckram requires more hand stitching than self-adhesive stiffener, and you will have to make your own pattern before you start. However, the end result has a softer look than one made with self-adhesive stiffener, and it should last longer because it can be cleaned.

The pelmet should be an eighth to a sixth of the length of the window – standard depths are 30-40cm (12-16in) at the deepest points. It must hide the track even at the highest points.

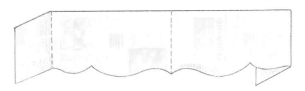

MAKING A PATTERN

1 Measuring up Measure the length of the shelf plus returns (short side ends). Cut a strip of paper this length by the required depth. Fold it in half to mark the centre and crease it to mark the position of the corners.

2 Drawing the shaped edge Open out the paper and draw the shape of the edge on to it. Work from the centre outwards, making sure repeated shapes are the same size and evenly spaced. The returns can be shaped or plain.

3 Cutting the shape Keep the paper folded while cutting out so that the shape will be symmetrical. Tape the pattern to the pelmet shelf to check the effect and adjust the outline if necessary.

MAKING A BUCKRAM PELMET

1 Cutting out Using the pattern as a guide, cut out one pelmet shape from buckram. Cut one pelmet piece from the main fabric, adding 2.5cm (1in) to outer edges. Cut out bump or iron-on interfacing adding 1.2cm (½in) to outer edges. Cut out lining adding 1cm (⅜in) to outer edges.

2 Attaching iron-on interfacing or bump Press iron-on interfacing centrally to wrong side of fabric. Pin bump centrally to fabric and work rows of lockstitch 25cm (10in) apart along pelmet.

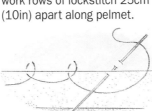

3 Attaching buckram Buckram is stiff to handle, so it is wise to use a strong, sharp needle and a thimble to protect your finger. Place buckram centrally on top of interfacing. Pin and tack through all layers. Clip into the fabric turnings at curves and corners, and trim away excess. Dampen the edges of the buckram and press the fabric turnings into place. For extra security, slipstitch the turned fabric to the buckram.

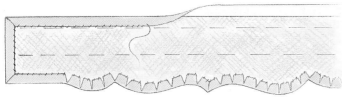

4 Adding trimmings Stitch or glue any trimmings of braid or fringing to the pelmet at this stage.

5 Adding lining Turn in 1cm (⅜in) to wrong side of lining. Clip and trim as necessary at curves, tack and press. If you are hanging the pelmet with Velcro, stitch the soft half of the strip along the top edge of right side of lining at this stage. Position lining, right side up, on top of buckram. Pin and slipstitch all round, catching lining to seam allowance of the main pelmet fabric. If using curtain rings, hand stitch in place at this stage. Then hang the pelmet.

SELF-ADHESIVE STIFFENERS

The self-adhesive stiffeners have a peel-off backing paper printed with either a pelmet shape or a grid which enables you to draw up your own design. They come in two forms. Single-sided stiffener has a self-adhesive front and the back is coated with velour which makes lining unnecessary. It comes in 30cm (12in) and 40cm (16in) widths. Double-sided stiffener has adhesive on both sides. It does need lining but gives a more professional finish. It comes in 30cm (12in), 40cm (16in) and 60cm (24in) widths.

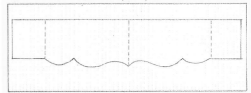

SHAPING ON THE GRID

Make a paper pattern for the pelmet as above. Mark the centre and position of the shelf returns on to the grid on the back of the stiffener, then draw up the design. When satisfied with the design, cut out the shape and make up the pelmet, following the instructions for using a pre-printed design on the following page.

Using Pre-printed Designs

The scalloped edge of this pelmet was cut out following the pre-printed Georgian pattern on the back of a strip of self-adhesive stiffener.

Pre-printed self-adhesive stiffeners offer a choice of designs – simply select the one that you want and cut it out, first centring the design on the width of the pelmet as explained below.

1 Measuring up Measure the pelmet shelf, plus the returns. With the design on the self-adhesive stiffener centred, mark the required length and returns. Check the design looks good from the front; you may need to reshape the pattern along the returns. Cut to length, then cut along the lower edge following the pattern lines.

2 Cutting fabric and lining Press the fabric, then position the stiffener to the wrong side. For patterned fabrics ensure the pattern is centred. Using chalk, draw around the stiffener. Cut out adding a 2.5cm (1in) seam allowance all round. With a directional fabric, if necessary join widths before cutting out pelmet shape.

3 Applying stiffener Starting at the centre of the strip of stiffener, lift and then cut through the centre of the backing. Peel back part of the backing then, using the chalk outline as a guide, position it adhesive side down to the wrong side of the fabric. Smooth the exposed adhesive surface to the fabric, making sure there are no wrinkles. Peel away the rest of the backing a little at a time, smoothing the adhesive down on to the fabric as you do so.

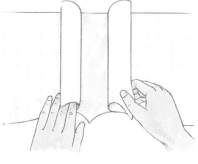

Finishing the Edges

Single sided self-adhesive stiffeners
Snip into seams to within 3mm (⅛in) of stiffener and turn edges over to wrong side. Glue in place. Alternatively, trim excess fabric close to edge of self-adhesive stiffener and stitch or glue braid along lower edge to finish. Attach Velcro or hooks as required.

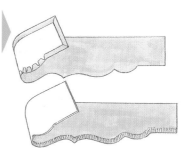

Double sided self-adhesive stiffeners
If using Velcro, sew the soft half to right side of lining 2.5cm (1in) from top edge. Press a 1.5cm (⅝in) turning to wrong side all around. With wrong sides together, smooth the lining on to the adhesive surface from the centre out and slipstitch lining to fabric. If using curtain rings, sew them at regular intervals round the top edge.

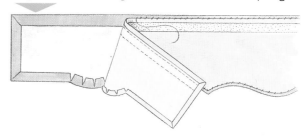

Curtain tracks, poles and rods

Tracks, poles and rods are a practical necessity, and a decorative addition to your window dressing.

Once you have decided on the style of curtains, you need to choose the right type of fitting for hanging them to look their best and suit the style of the window. Whatever your requirements, there is a track or pole suitable for the task, with options for plain through to very decorative solutions. Ask yourself:

❖ **Are the curtains light, medium or heavyweight?** Check that your choice of track or pole is strong enough to take their weight.

❖ **Where am I going to fix the track?** Make sure that the track you choose can be attached to the ceiling or window frame instead of the wall, if necessary.

❖ **Is the window in a bay?** Find out whether the track is flexible enough to be bent round the angles, or if the poles or rods come with angled connections or curved joints to carry them round the corners.

❖ **Will I need a pelmet or valance to hide the track?** Not necessarily, if you hang the curtains from a pole or a concealed or decorative track, or make sure that the track blends with the paintwork in the background.

❖ **Do I want to hang nets or a blind, and/or a valance with the curtains?** If so, look out for special dual or triple track systems that are designed to create a stylish layered look at a window.

❖ **Am I going to pull the curtains by hand or with cords?** There are many corded tracks and poles that make pulling the curtains effortlessly smooth, without damaging the curtains.

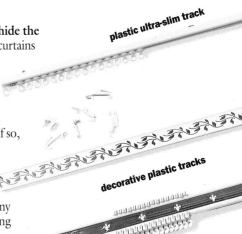

plastic corded track

plastic ultra-slim track

decorative plastic tracks

heavy duty metal track

concealed metal ceiling mounted track

metal combination track

ruche track with cord guides

basic plastic track

Tracks

Tracks are made from plastic or metal. They can be plain, coloured or decorated, and corded or uncorded. When buying your track, allow an extra 22.5cm (9in) on each side of the window so that you can pull the curtains right back.

Most tracks are supplied with brackets, screws and wallplugs for fitting them to the wall or ceiling, along with a range of accessories, including end stops to prevent the curtains falling off the track, gliders with integrated hooks, or runners and separate hooks, depending on the style of track. Spare components, like extra gliders, brackets, finials, cording sets and valance tracks, are available if you wish to modify your track system later on.

Some tracks have crossover arms so that the curtains overlap at their leading edges, helping to cut out light and reduce draughts. Avoid crossover arms for very heavy curtains, as the bulky fabric will make it difficult to close them.

Basic tracks are suitable for hanging sheers and light to mediumweight curtains. They are available in a range of standard lengths that can be cut to size using a small hacksaw, and are easy to fit to walls or ceilings.

Combination tracks have two or three tracks to carry the main curtain plus a valance and/or a sheer curtain or blind. Many come with cording systems. Separate *valance tracks* can also be fitted in front of a compatible single curtain track, or put up on independent brackets.

Concealed tracks are suitable for curtains with deep headings. The runners for holding the curtain hooks hang down below the track. The exposed front of the track can be papered, covered in fabric or painted to suit the rest of the room.

Heavy duty metal tracks are designed for medium to heavyweight curtains. Some are expandable, and easily adjusted to fit the window. Most come with cording systems. Steel tracks that have to be angled around bays or curved areas should be installed professionally.

Multipurpose tracks can be wall or ceiling mounted, and bent round bow windows. They have front mounted gliders with integrated hooks and rings, allowing you to hang a separate lining behind the curtain.

Ruche track has special cord guides and in-built hooks for hanging Austrian, festoon and Roman blinds neatly.

Ultra-slim tracks are neat and easy to bend. They are ideal for carrying nets and lightweight curtains, or frills round cots and dressing tables.

> ### TIP
> #### GLIDE SMOOTHLY
> To keep your track looking good and working smoothly, wipe it over occasionally using a soft cloth and some mild detergent. Allow it to dry and then spray a little silicone-based furniture polish to the running surface.

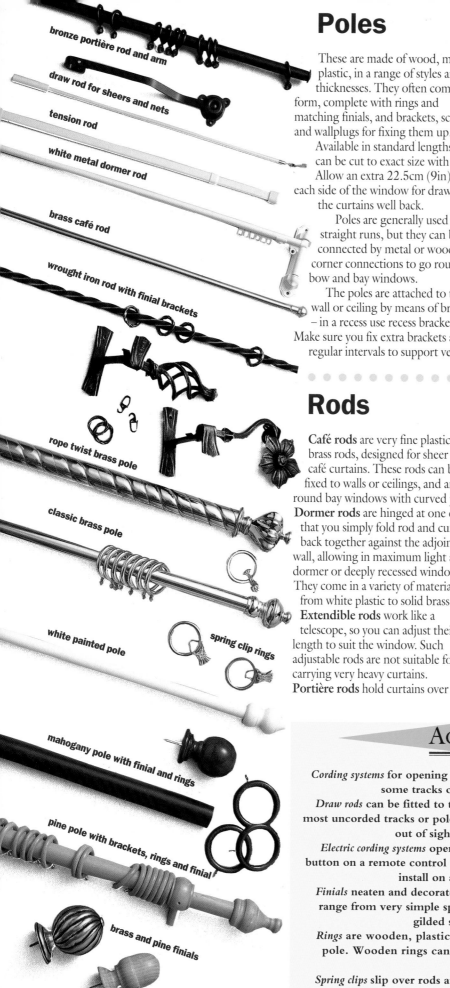

Poles

These are made of wood, metal or plastic, in a range of styles and thicknesses. They often come in kit form, complete with rings and matching finials, and brackets, screws and wallplugs for fixing them up.

Available in standard lengths, they can be cut to exact size with a saw. Allow an extra 22.5cm (9in) on each side of the window for drawing the curtains well back.

Poles are generally used for straight runs, but they can be connected by metal or wooden corner connections to go round bow and bay windows.

The poles are attached to the wall or ceiling by means of brackets – in a recess use recess brackets. Make sure you fix extra brackets at regular intervals to support very long poles or those carrying heavy, interlined curtains.

Metal poles can be made of heavy brass or iron, or more commonly lighter weight smooth or reeded (ridged) aluminium or steel in bright brass, black, white or ivory finishes.
Plastic poles are an inexpensive solution for supporting light to mediumweight curtains.
Wooden poles come in a range of natural wood shades and in plain colours, such as black and white. You can buy unvarnished poles and paint them to match your room scheme.
Concealed track poles, available in brass and wood finishes, look like poles but work like tracks, with simulated half rings that run smoothly on nylon gliders slotted into the back of the pole. They are frequently pre-corded.

Rods

Café rods are very fine plastic or brass rods, designed for sheer or café curtains. These rods can be fixed to walls or ceilings, and angled round bay windows with curved joints.
Dormer rods are hinged at one end so that you simply fold rod and curtain back together against the adjoining wall, allowing in maximum light at a dormer or deeply recessed window. They come in a variety of materials, from white plastic to solid brass.
Extendible rods work like a telescope, so you can adjust their length to suit the window. Such adjustable rods are not suitable for carrying very heavy curtains.
Portière rods hold curtains over external doors to keep out draughts. The hinged end of the rod is fitted to the door frame, while the other end is attached to the top edge of the door. The curtain lifts up as the door opens.
Tension rods are fine plastic rods with an internal spring-loading mechanism to hold them in place across a window recess. They are good for hanging light and sheer curtains.
Valance rods are designed to hold a valance in front of the curtain heading. They are smooth-faced, deep rods fixed to brackets at each end of the curtain track. The rod is threaded through a casing along the top of the valance, which is then ruched up to create a gathered heading.

ACCESSORIES

Cording systems for opening and closing the curtains are provided with some tracks or can be installed separately.
Draw rods can be fitted to the leading ring or hook of the curtain on most uncorded tracks or poles. When the curtain is closed the rods hang out of sight behind the curtain edge.
Electric cording systems open and close the curtains at the touch of a button on a remote control unit. They are expensive to buy but easy to install on any corded track or pole.
Finials neaten and decorate the ends of the tracks and poles. Shapes range from very simple spheres and acorns to ornately carved and gilded spearheads or animals.
Rings are wooden, plastic or metal to match or contrast with the pole. Wooden rings can be painted to pick out a colour in the curtains.
Spring clips slip over rods and poles to grip sheers and light curtains.

bronze portière rod and arm

draw rod for sheers and nets

tension rod

white metal dormer rod

brass café rod

wrought iron rod with finial brackets

rope twist brass pole

classic brass pole

spring clip rings

white painted pole

mahogany pole with finial and rings

pine pole with brackets, rings and finial

brass and pine finials

walnut draw rod

DECORATED CURTAIN POLES

Turn a plain curtain pole into a designer original by decorating it with a paint finish, or cover it with wallpaper to match other furnishings in the room.

By decorating a curtain pole and fittings to complement the curtain fabric and the overall style of your room, you can add a dash of individuality to window dressings. Starting with a basic wooden, metal or plastic pole, you can use paint and wallpaper or a range of decorative paint techniques and painted patterns to ring the changes and improve the look of ordinary, inexpensive fittings.

Plain, varnished or ready-painted wooden poles provide the ideal surface for paint, although with thorough preparation and the right paints you can also decorate plastic and metal poles. Broken colour effects, such

as sponging, ragging and colourwashing, are usually worked using several colours, giving you the opportunity to match colours from your curtains or their surroundings. You can create new looks with all-over paint effects or painted stripes, or highlight different details such as the finials, curtain rings and support fittings with individual blocks of colour.

For a completely coordinated look, consider covering the curtain pole with pattern, using a wallpaper to match the curtains. Or, for a really ambitious project, try hand-painting a design – the possibilities are all there to create your own small masterpiece.

Wooden curtain poles and fittings provide the perfect starting point for a range of decorative effects using paint and wallpaper.

PAINTING A CURTAIN POLE

It is important to choose the appropriate paint for the type of curtain pole. Quick-drying water-based paint such as silk or vinyl emulsion/latex is the most practical choice for wooden curtain poles. You can speed the drying time with a hairdryer, and protect the paint with a coat of clear varnish. Use enamel paint to give plastic poles a resilient finish. On brass and other metal curtain poles, use car spray paint, metal-finish paint or enamel paint. These paints are also suitable for wooden poles.

Take the curtain fabric as inspiration for the colours for your pole. One starting point is to paint the pole in a colour picked out from the fabric background then, aiming to follow the same colour balance as the print, paint the rings and fittings in various colours to match. Alternatively, copy the fabric print on to the pole – stripes are particularly effective – or decorate it with a complementary paint effect.

1 Preparing surfaces Use fine sandpaper to rub all over a wooden, metal or plastic pole and its fittings to key the surfaces and to remove any flaky paint, varnish or surface grease.

2 Hand-painting a pole To paint a pole with a base coat, or with one solid colour, balance the pole between two chair backs and simply twist it round as you paint. Allow the paint to dry before applying a second coat or special paint effect.

3 Painting the fittings On newspaper, paint the brackets and end stops in sections, each side at a time. Hold each ring by the curtain-hook ring and paint first one side, leave to dry flat, then the other side. Or thread the rings on to a length of string pinned to a shelf, holding them in place with knots, and paint as they hang. Repeat for a second coat, decorative paint effect or stripes.

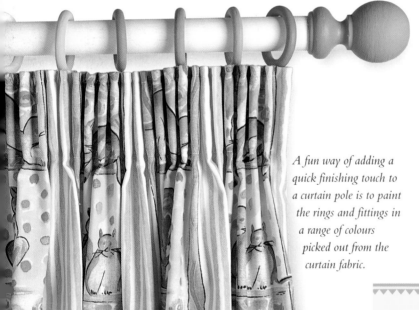

A fun way of adding a quick finishing touch to a curtain pole is to paint the rings and fittings in a range of colours picked out from the curtain fabric.

TIP
SPRAY PAINTING
To spray paint a plastic or wooden pole, work in a well ventilated space and mask off the surrounding area with old newspapers before you start. Following the instructions on the spray can, copy steps 2 and 3 of *Painting a Curtain Pole* to paint the pole and fittings. Always make a point of cleaning the spray nozzle after use.

4 Varnishing For water-based paints, finish the curtain pole with one or two coats of polyurethane varnish, applying it in the same way as the paint.

PAINTING STRIPES

It is quite simple to paint a curtain pole with classic stripes, worked vertically, horizontally or diagonally, to match striped curtains or as a finishing touch for plain drapes. Then you can paint the rings and fittings to blend with the stripes or the fabric background.

Before marking on the stripes, prepare and paint the pole in a solid colour or paint effect, following *Painting a Curtain Pole*, to serve as a background for the stripes. Use the lightest colour of your striped design as the background and overpaint darker coloured stripes.

Besides the basic tools and materials given on the previous page, you also need a tape measure and pencil to mark the stripes and low-tack masking tape to mask them off. You might find a coloured sketch of the stripes a helpful reference.

Painting vertical stripes Use a tape measure and pencil to mark the stripe sequence on to the pole. Wrap masking tape round the pole to mark the edges of the first set of stripes. Paint between the masking tape with a sponge or a small paint brush. Leave to dry, then add another coat if required. When the paint is dry, gently peel away the masking tape. Repeat to paint different coloured stripes.

Painting diagonal stripes Starting at one end of the pole, hold the masking tape diagonally to the pole end and twist the pole so that the tape winds itself round in a regular spiral. The spaces between the tape form the stripes. If you want the stripes to be closer or further apart, re-position and re-wind the tape. When you are happy with the effect, check that the tape is pressed flat all round so no colour seeps underneath, and paint between the masking tape. To create stripes within stripes, tape the pole again, cutting the tape into narrower strips if necessary. Paint as before.

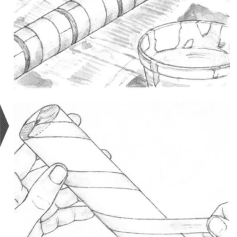

Use masking tape to apply paint in horizontal or vertical stripes, or for a softer finish try a paint effect – the chalky pink tones of the colour-rubbed pole blend admirably with the curtains.

Painting horizontal stripes These are most suited to large diameter poles. Starting along the centre front, use a tape measure and pencil to mark the position of the first stripe. Run masking tape along the edges of the stripe, trimming the tape into narrow strips if necessary to accommodate closely spaced stripes. Mark these in the same way and paint between the tapes. When the paint is dry, carefully peel off the tapes.

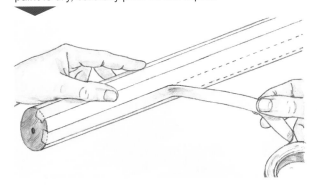

PAINTING PATTERNS

If your curtain fabric has a distinctive pattern motif, you can copy the design on to the pole and fittings. Paint the pole, then hold a tracing of the design in place with sticky tape. Slip well worn dressmakers' carbon paper underneath the tracing paper to transfer the design. Paint the design with watercolour brushes. If you need to mix paints to get the desired shades, use small jars with lids to stop the paints drying out.

WALLPAPER-TRIMMED POLES

To make the most of coordinated ranges, cover a pole with wallpaper to match your fabric and paint the fittings the same colour as the wallpaper background. As a finishing touch decorate the finials and other fittings with a decoupage of motifs cut out from the wallpaper. Finish the pole with a coat of varnish to protect the paper and create a sheen.

In addition to the materials for *Painting a Curtain Pole* you need wallpaper and wallpaper adhesive, or contact paper.

1 Measuring up Measure round the circumference of the curtain pole and mark the measurement across the wallpaper. Position the cutting lines so that motifs or pattern details are centred on the pole. Cut out the wallpaper along the marked lines – this piece will be placed centrally on the curtain pole. Cut another two pieces to match the pattern at the side edges. If necessary, cut more pieces to cover the pole.

2 Positioning the wallpaper Mark the centre of the pole and lightly mark the centre back of the first piece of wallpaper. Paste the back of the paper and smooth it on to the pole, aligning the centre marks. Paste the other pieces and butt them up to the first piece on each side, trimming the paper at the pole ends as necessary. To seal the surface of non-vinyl papers to prevent varnish later discolouring the paper, brush a thin coat of paste over the right side of the wallpaper. Leave to dry.

3 Decorating the fittings Cut small motifs from the wallpaper, making sure they are not too large to fit smoothly over curves. To ease the motifs to shape, cut small snips into the paper and overlap the cut edges to fit. You can also overlap several small motifs to give an impression of the main design. Paste and smooth the motifs on to the fittings. Brush over them with paste to seal the surface as in step 2. When dry, protect with varnish.

This floral print is an ideal candidate for a decoupage project. The pole is wrapped with wallpaper and the motif on the finial is formed by overlapping small details cut from the paper.

PLAITED TIEBACKS

Sweep back your curtains in style with plaited tiebacks.
Mix and match colours and patterns in a three or five-stranded plait
that adds a stately flourish to your decor.

Tiebacks are an attractive and practical accessory for curtains, adding panache and a dash of colour to a room. Plaited tiebacks are made by simply braiding together padded tubes of fabric. They're a versatile option, as you can make them from a combination of different fabrics to link with the rest of the room. They're also a great way to use up favourite fabric scraps.

The colour and style of the curtains may suggest the most appropriate fabrics for the tiebacks, or you can let your imagination run riot with some completely contrasting colours.

You can use almost any type of fabric to make the tiebacks, as long as it is not so lightweight or openly woven that the wadding shows through. If your heart is set on using delicate sheers, plaiting together unpadded fabric tubes makes a pretty and original variation.

A plump plaited tieback weaves together a selection of fabrics that echoes other colours in the room. Placed one-third of the way up the French doors, the tieback draws the curtain well back from the fine view outside.

MAKING A PLAITED TIEBACK

Plaited tiebacks are made from tubes of fabric filled with either wadding or thick soft cord then woven together. For a chunkier plait cut wider pieces of fabric to make thicker strands. Hold the curtains to one side of the window using a tape measure to gauge the best position for the tiebacks.

1 Cutting the fabric Fix a cup hook into the wall or window frame at the desired tieback height. Hold a tape measure loosely around the drawn-back curtain at this point, and note the length. Add half this length again to allow for shrinkage due to plaiting. Cut three 12.5cm (5in) wide fabric strips to this length.

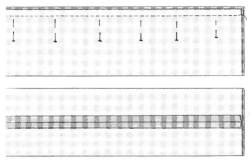

Pretty and practical, a plaited tieback in toning colours and different patterns adds accent and form to a simple unlined curtain.

2 Making the fabric tubes With right sides together, fold each fabric strip in half lengthways and pin together. Taking a 6mm (¼in) seam allowance, stitch the long raw edge. Centre the seam and press open. Trim the seams and turn each tube right side out.

3 Padding the tubes Cut a piece of wadding to the length and width of each stitched tube. Push the wadding into each tube to fill its length. Turn in the short edges of the fabric and slipstitch to close.

4 Plaiting the tubes Place the tubes side-by-side with the seams at the back. Overlap the ends and handstitch them firmly together. Braid the tubes together as for a conventional plait. At the end of the plait, overlap the three ends and hand stitch them together.

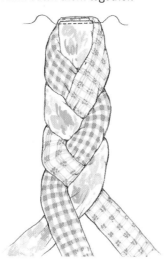

5 Finishing the plait ends Fold the raw ends of the plait to the back and slipstitch in place. Alternatively, cut bias binding 2cm (¾in) longer than the plait width and stitch over the plait ends. Stitch a curtain ring to the centre back of each plait end. Place the tieback around the curtain and slip the rings over the cup hook.

A FIVE-STRANDED PLAIT

Make five padded tubes to the required length, following steps 1–3 above. Overlap the tubes at one end and stitch them together. Weave the left tube over the next tube and under the centre tube. Weave the right tube over the next tube and under the centre tube. Repeat these two steps to the end of the tubes and stitch the ends together.

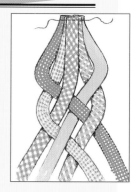

VELVET ROSES

Stitch a posy of sumptuous velvet roses as a charming detail for curtain tiebacks, a valance or swagged heading. Strips of fabric can quickly be folded and gathered into everlasting blooms.

Plush and sumptuous, velvet roses are a welcome softening influence on many styles of window dressing. Use a mixed posy to add a whimsical touch to a classic tailored tieback as shown above, or space individual blooms across a pelmet to break its formal lines. The roses also enhance softer window draperies, giving them ultra-feminine appeal but with a sophisticated note. Apply them singly across the top of a gathered valance as an alternative to fabric rosettes, or use them to catch up swags of fabric in a casually draped arrangement.

The roses and leaves featured here are made from curtain velvet, which is stiff enough to hold its shape, but with enough flexibility to be easily manageable and to form soft folds when gathered. Curtain velvet is available in a wide range of shades. You can keep to natural rose colours – blend dusky pinks and delicate peaches with warm golds, or make a stronger statement with rich scarlet hues or splashes of vivid orange; keep to dark green leaves to continue the natural theme. Alternatively, create sumptuous, fantasy effects with blue, black or purple velvet roses teamed with gold leaves. Whichever colour combinations you choose, make sure they tone with the curtain and tieback fabric and form a pleasing balance.

A posy of velvet roses in dusky pinks and warm gold is a fitting embellishment for a floral curtain tieback, whose tones they echo perfectly. Green velvet leaves frame the blooms and echo the natural theme.

MAKING A POSY OF ROSES

The posy of roses is made up of open blooms and rosebuds, surrounded by a few velvet leaves. For a good sized tieback posy, you need three or four open roses, three or four rosebuds and four or five leaves, using a combination of two or three toning velvets for the flowers, together with your chosen leaf shade. Remember to double the numbers if you want a matching tieback for each side of the window. A 120 x 50cm (47½ x 20in) piece of velvet is sufficient for seven roses and four or five rosebuds, and a 50 x 25cm (20 x 10in) piece makes several leaves.

The flowers are made from strips of velvet cut on the bias, folded and then gathered up into a coil shape. Cutting on the bias helps the roses curl round in a more natural way. The rosebuds are made in the same way as the open flowers, but from smaller and more tightly gathered strips. The velvet leaves are cut from a double layer of velvet, with a piece of lightweight wadding sandwiched in-between to give them added body. Their edges are neatened with zigzag stitch, and each has a zigzagged vein detail down the centre. To form the posy, the flowers and leaves are stitched together then mounted on a toning felt base.

MAKING OPEN ROSES

1 Cutting out Use the long ruler and dressmakers' pencil to measure and mark 10cm (4in) wide strips diagonally across the fabric bias – one for each rose. Cut out the strips and, if necessary, trim to 70cm (27½in) long.

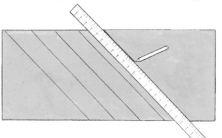

2 Shaping the strip Fold one strip in half lengthways, wrong sides together. Use a dressmakers' pencil to curve both ends of the strip as shown. Trim along the marked curves.

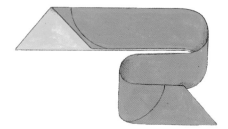

3 Stitching the strip Thread a needle with buttonhole thread or a double length of sewing thread and knot one end. Work a long running stitch along the raw base edges of the strip, including the curved ends, about 6mm (¼in) from edge.

4 Gathering up the strip Pull the loose thread end at one end of the strip to slightly gather the fabric at the opposite end. Starting at the gathered end, begin rolling up the strip to form the centre of the rose. With a needle and fresh length of sewing thread, secure the rolled-up centre with a couple of stitches through the base.

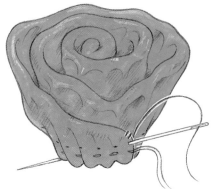

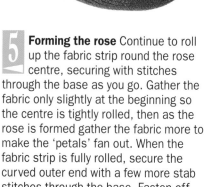

5 Forming the rose Continue to roll up the fabric strip round the rose centre, securing with stitches through the base as you go. Gather the fabric only slightly at the beginning so the centre is tightly rolled, then as the rose is formed gather the fabric more to make the 'petals' fan out. When the fabric strip is fully rolled, secure the curved outer end with a few more stab stitches through the base. Fasten off the sewing and gathering threads. Repeat steps 2-5 for each rose.

MAKING ROSEBUDS

1 Cutting out the strips For each rosebud, measure and mark out 8cm (3¼in) wide bias strips, as for *Making Open Roses*, step 1. Trim the strips to 32cm (12½in) long if necessary. Fold, shape and run a gathering thread along each strip as for *Making Open Roses*, steps 2 and 3.

2 Forming the rosebud Roll up the strip very tightly to form the centre of the bud, hardly gathering the fabric at all, and secure with a few stab stitches through the base. Continue rolling up the strip, pulling slightly on the gathering thread to help compress the fabric at the base of the bud, but still keeping the petals tightly packed. At the end of the strip, gather the fabric a little more so the outer petals just start to spread. Secure with a few stitches. Fasten off the threads.

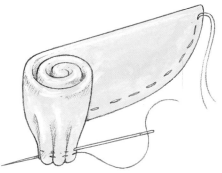

MAKING LEAVES

1 Preparing the fabric Fold the rectangle of green velvet in half and cut along the fold. Sandwich a piece of lightweight wadding between the velvet pieces, right sides out. Pin and tack the three layers together across the centre of the fabric.

2 Marking out the leaves Trace the leaf template on to stiff cardboard and cut it out. Use a dressmakers' pencil to draw round it on to the velvet and wadding sandwich, once for each leaf required. Mark in the central vein on each leaf.

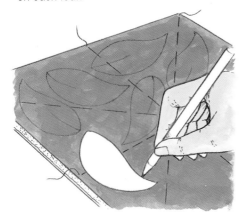

3 Stitching the leaves Using a close, wide zigzag stitch and beginning at the base of each leaf, stitch along one side. As you approach the leaf tip, alter the stitch width to a narrower setting to give a finer outline. Stitch round the tip then reset the stitch width to its original size and continue down the other side to the leaf base. Stitch the vein in the same way, narrowing the top to a fine point.

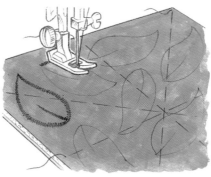

4 Cutting out Use sharp scissors to cut around each leaf, taking care not to snip any threads. Rub around the edges to loosen any fibres, then give the leaves a final trim.

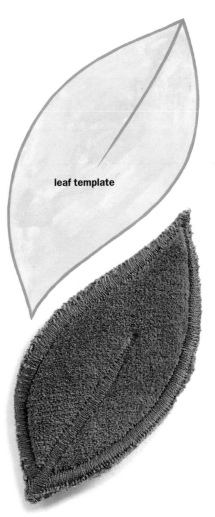

leaf template

GROUPING THE FLOWERS

1 Arranging the flowers Bunch the roses and buds together, forming a fairly tight group. Place the leaves randomly round the outside, temporarily pinning them in place. When you're happy with the arrangement, hold it against the tieback to judge the effect.

2 Stitching the group Starting with the flowers and buds at the centre of the group, stitch all the flowers together taking stab stitches through the bases. Stitch the base ends of the leaves in place just under the flower bases, so they fan out.

3 Covering the base Cut a piece of felt large enough to cover the base of the posy, and glue it in place. Trim the felt to within 6mm (¼in) of the base edge, then slipstitch it in place round the edges so it just covers all the raw edges. Slipstitch the posy in place on the tieback.

◀ *For a casual and quick variation on the theme, you can make fabric roses by simply rolling a velvet tube into a coil, twisting the fabric as you go and securing with small stitches. Here honey gold velvet roses are teamed with rich green leaves to echo the curtain's sumptuous colour mix.*

▶ *A small wicker basket brimming with velvet roses makes a charming window-ledge ornament.*

FABRIC OPTIONS

Try experimenting with different fabrics and sizes of rose to add a new slant to their impact. Large floral patterns or tiny sprig prints give a fresh, country feel to the flowers and combine well with both formal satin or velvet curtains and casual checks or stripes. Dainty blooms stitched from finest voile and organdie in pale pastel hues give fairy-tale appeal, and strike a good balance on fine fabric draperies.

ALTERNATIVE LEAF DESIGN

To make the neat, self-fabric leaves, use the template on the previous page to cut two fabric leaves, adding 3mm (⅛in) for seams all round, and one fine interlining leaf; adapt the template size if desired. With right sides together, pin and stitch round the main fabric leaves, leaving an opening in the base.

Trim and turn right side out. Slide the interfacing inside the leaf, covering the seam allowances, and slipstitch closed. Make a tiny tuck in the centre of each leaf and catch together at the base with a few stitches.

▲ *Clusters of roses styled from fine, translucent fabrics attract the eye to the heading of an unashamedly pretty valance. This sweet arrangement dresses a plain semi-sheer fabric to give it a delicate, feminine look. Group the roses together in a random colour arrangement for the best effect.*

◀ *A floral chintz drape and matching formal tieback are given added country cottage appeal by an informal scattering of fabric roses. Flowers to match the drapes are balanced with toning checked blooms and striped and checked leaves – all made from remnants of fabrics used elsewhere in the room.*

TIP

QUICK CUTTING OUT

If making several roses from two or more different fabrics, you can save marking up and cutting out time by layering the fabrics on top of each other and marking up the top layer only; use a rotary cutter, metal rule and cutting mat to cut the strips through all layers.

▶ *Simplicity itself, a softly draped voile curtain is held by a matching tieback trimmed with a posy of voile roses. For subtle textural interest, choose the same fabrics for curtains, tieback and flowers.*

CURTAIN HOLDBACKS

*In wood or wrought iron, lavishly gilded or covered
with fabric, holdbacks make a handsome change to fabric or cord
tiebacks for holding back your curtains.*

L ike fabric or cord tiebacks, holdbacks are fixed at each side of the window so that you can gracefully sweep the curtains back over them. Made in wood, metal, plastic or resin, they either have a shaped end piece or are hooked round to prevent the curtains slipping forwards. As well as being an attractive alternative to tiebacks, holdbacks are easier to use as you don't need to tie and untie them – you simply slip the curtains in place behind them.

Curtain holdbacks are becoming increasingly popular, so there is a surprising selection on offer at your local department store or home improvement centre. They range from simple, inexpensive designs to exquisitely crafted pieces – like the antique-effect, gilded and decoupaged holdbacks shown on the right. You can easily customize plain holdbacks yourself by gilding, staining or painting them, or you can cover them with fabric as shown overleaf.

▲ *Lightweight voile curtains drape gracefully over gilt holdbacks and fall in soft folds to the floor. The holdbacks' classic shape and design is perfect for this elegant setting.*

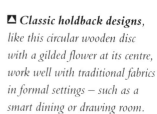

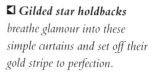

◢ Classic holdback designs, like this circular wooden disc with a gilded flower at its centre, work well with traditional fabrics in formal settings — such as a smart dining or drawing room.

◣ Gilded star holdbacks breathe glamour into these simple curtains and set off their gold stripe to perfection.

▶ Lavishly gilded, this leaf-shaped holdback made from moulded resin is a handsome and apt choice for sumptuous floral drapes. Its curving arm is deep enough to hold back the folds of even the thickest interlined curtains.

◥ Make an impact with strikingly shaped holdbacks in solid wrought iron — like the classic fleur de lys motif shown here.

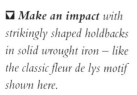

◢ A swirl of wrought iron provides a dramatic contrast in colour and texture to the flimsy sheer drape it encloses.

◣ For a soft variation on the look, cover a plain holdback with fabric to match your curtain. For added effect, you can finish it with a twisted cord trim as shown here.

A guide to fabric blinds

Consider fabric blinds as an attractive and economical alternative to curtains.

Blinds are a versatile way of covering windows to provide shade and privacy, either hung on their own or teamed with curtains. They prove especially useful where a window is awkwardly placed or there is not much room around it for hanging curtains.

The styles range from plain, streamlined roller blinds to the extravagant swags of romantic festoon blinds or Austrian blinds. Choose a boldly patterned fabric for a bright modern look, or muted colours and subtle patterns for softer effects. Most blinds end up being cheaper than curtains because they need less fabric.

The main types of fabric blinds are listed below, together with diagrams of the front and back to show how they are constructed. (The second diagram for the roller blind illustrates the special roller fitting.)

Fabric blinds can be bought ready made, made to measure, or you can make them yourself.

Roller blinds

These are flat blinds where the fabric winds round a roller at the top. A spring-loaded mechanism allows the blind to be raised or lowered by pulling a cord. The lower edge is held straight by a wooden slat in a casing.

To make a roller blind, buy stiffened fabric, or stiffen lightweight, closely woven fabric with a liquid or spray stiffener. The straight lines of the blind can be softened with braid or fringing, or by shaping the lower edge into scallops or zigzags.

Festoon blinds

These look similar to Austrian blinds when they are raised, but keep their swagged appearance, even when fully let down, because special festoon blind tape is used to gather the blinds vertically into flounces.

Festoon blinds are often made from soft, lightweight and sheer fabrics, and are either used on their own or teamed with curtains. Frills may be added around the edges to enhance the pretty effect.

Austrian blinds

An Austrian blind gathers into flounced panels when raised, but on lowering it hangs straight like a curtain, with only a few soft folds along the bottom. It is gathered horizontally at the top with curtain heading tape, and raised by a series of cords threaded through rings or loops on the back. The blind is hung from a ruche track or standard track attached to a batten.

Austrian blinds are made from furnishing cottons, and look effective in sheer fabrics.

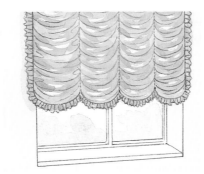

Roman blinds

When lowered, these lie flat against the window, but fold into neat horizontal pleats on raising. The lower edge is kept straight with a wooden slat slotted into a casing. Often, especially on wide windows, extra horizontal slats are fitted to define the pleats.

Roman blinds are raised and lowered by means of cords threaded through rings attached at regular intervals on the back. Most types of furnishing fabric can be used, except sheers. Roman blinds are often lined.

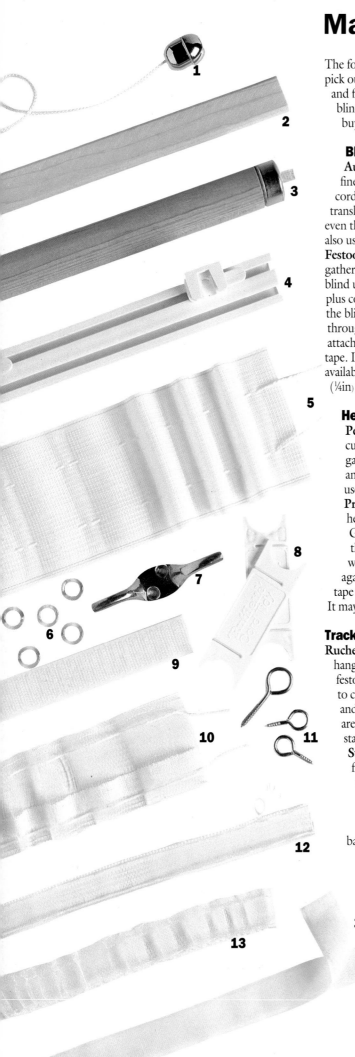

Materials for making blinds

The following guide will help you pick out the specialist tape, track and fittings to make and hang the blind of your choice. You need to buy a kit for a roller blind.

Blind tapes

Austrian blind tape (12) has fine raised loops for carrying the cords that raise the blind. Special translucent tape is almost invisible, even through sheers. This tape is also used to create Roman blinds. **Festoon blind tape** (13) has gathering threads for pulling the blind up into soft, permanent folds, plus cords for raising and lowering the blind. These are threaded through loops or tiny rings (6) attached along one edge of the tape. If blind tapes are not readily available in your area, use 6mm (¼in) or 12mm (½in) curtain rings.

Heading tapes

Pencil pleat tape or standard curtain tape is suitable for gathering the top of Austrian and festoon blinds. On sheers use a translucent tape (10). **Press 'n' Drape** pencil pleat heading tape (5) is used with Grip tape (9). It is sewn along the top of sheer and light-weight blinds, and pressed against the self-adhesive Grip tape stuck on above the window. It may be hard to find in the USA.

Tracks

Ruche track (4) is made for hanging Roman, Austrian and festoon blinds. It has cord holders to channel the cords that raise and lower the blind. The blinds are attached to the track with standard curtain hooks.

Standard curtain track is best fixed to a wooden batten when hanging blinds, so that screw eyes can be fitted underneath to thread the cords through. Screw the batten straight to the wall or secure it with angle brackets. If the track is already in place, fix screw eyes into the window frame, or a batten below the track.

Fixings

Wooden batten As well as modifying standard curtain tracks for carrying blinds, a wall-fixed batten can be used for anchoring a Roman blind. The fabric is either stapled to the batten or hung from it on touch-and-close fastening. **Touch-and-close fastening** (14) Used to attach Roman blinds to wooden battens, when one half of the tape is stuck to the front of the batten and the other half is sewn to the top of the blind, which is then just pressed in place on the batten. **Net rods** Lightweight, permanently lowered blinds can be threaded on to net rods or covered curtain wire.

Kits

Roman, Austrian and **festoon** blind kits come in two sizes, for windows up to 122cm (48in) wide and those up to 183cm (72in). They contain everything you need except the track and the fabric. If kits are not readily available in your area, improvise using a standard curtain track and heading tape, and split or transparent curtain rings. **Roller blind** kits include a wooden roller (3) with a spring mechanism which you can cut to fit your window, a wooden slat (2) to slip into the bottom casing and hold it straight, two holding brackets, a pin end and a cap to fit over the free end of the roller – everything you need except the fabric. Some also come with a cord and pull.

Useful fittings

Pulls (1) neaten the knotted ends of the blind cords. They are made of wood, plastic, china or metal and can be found in novelty designs shaped like animals or flowers. **Cleats** (7) secured beside the window provide anchorage for the blind cords to keep the blind raised. They come in a range of sizes, and are made of coated metal or brass. **Cord tidies** (8) hold the heading tape cords together and keep them out of the way by slotting into the heading tape. **Screw eyes** (11) are fixed to the underside of the wooden batten when standard curtain track is used for hanging blinds to carry the blind cords.

ROLLER BLINDS

An attractive and economical alternative to curtains, roller blinds are easy to make and fit. You can use them to ensure privacy or as sunshades, or simply as a decorative addition to curtains.

In confined spaces and on small windows, roller blinds make an excellent substitute for curtains. They can also be teamed up effectively with curtains to keep out the sun or to provide privacy in the same way as net curtains.

A roller blind is the simplest and most economical of blinds to make, requiring the minimum of fabric and sewing. Since the blind lies flat against the window, you only need the same amount of fabric as the area of the window, plus a very little extra at the top and bottom.

Kits in many sizes are available from department stores and home improvement centres. They come with simple assembly instructions that should be followed carefully. Specially treated stiffened and spongeable blind fabric is easy to find, and comes in a variety of widths up to 175cm (69in) This means that you can cover practically any window without making unsightly joins. For economy you can cut stiffened fabric sideways as well, since it does not have a grain.

You can stiffen furnishing fabric yourself for making a blind in the same fabric as the curtains or to coordinate with other soft furnishings. The stiffening solution also prevents the fabric from fraying. Suitable stiffening solutions may be purchased at craft/fabric stores. Fabric used for making blinds must be closely woven, firm and colourfast; thin fabrics crease too easily and thick ones will not roll satisfactorily.

Roller blinds can be as plain or as pretty as you wish; the simplest are made of plain fabric with a lath at the base, while the most lavish make a feature of the window, with patterned fabrics, shaped edging, tasselled trimmings and elaborate corded pulls. Details on making a roller blind with a shaped edge are given in the next section.

A cutout border, created from a stiffened panel of curtain fabric, makes a pretty edging for a plain blind. The gingham band hides the wooden slat along the lower edge.

MAKING A ROLLER BLIND

Follow step 5 to calculate the amount of fabric required. To join widths of fabric, allow 1.5cm (⅝in) on each width for overlapping joins and position the joins at equal intervals across the blind. Remember to allow extra too for matching the pattern when joining widths, or when you plan to make a number of blinds that will hang next to each other.

Generally a blind is hung inside the window recess (**A**) so that it can be combined with curtains hung in front. If it is to be used alone, it can be hung outside the recess (**B**) to make the window look wider.

Roller blind kits come complete with the roller, brackets, spring loaded winding mechanism, wooden slat, cord and pull toggle.

1 **Measuring up for the blind kit** Measure the width of the window recess. To ensure light won't come in round the edges when hanging the blind in front of the recess, add 10cm (4in) to the measurement for an overlap on either side. Buy a roller blind kit of the exact measurement or the next size up which can be cut to fit.

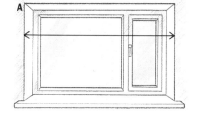
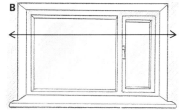

YOU WILL NEED

- ❖ ROLLER BLIND KIT
- ❖ STEEL MEASURING TAPE
- ❖ LEVEL
- ❖ BRADAWL or DRILL, MASONRY BIT and WALLPLUGS
- ❖ SCREWDRIVER
- ❖ SMALL SAW and HAMMER
- ❖ ROLLER BLIND FABRIC or FABRIC plus STIFFENING AGENT
- ❖ ROTARY CUTTING WHEEL or CRAFT KNIFE
- ❖ STEEL RULE
- ❖ MATCHING THREAD or FABRIC GLUE
- ❖ DECORATIVE TRIMMING (optional)
- ❖ ADHESIVE TAPE
- ❖ TACKS or STAPLE GUN

Sheer white curtains and a simple pelmet provide a crisp, light frame for a patterned roller blind. Normally, when printed fabrics are rolled up, the plain side of the fabric will be visible on the roller – to prevent this, reverse the position of the brackets so that the fabric drop hides the roller.

2 Fixing brackets Follow manufacturer's instructions for fitting brackets, checking first that they are level. Use a bradawl, screws and screwdriver for fixing into wood; a drill, wallplugs, screws and a screwdriver for masonry.

Inside the recess, position brackets close to the sides, at least 3cm (1¼in) from the top of the recess or ceiling to allow for rolled fabric.

Outside the recess, position brackets at least 5cm (2in) from the recess edges and 5cm (2in) above it to prevent light showing round the top and sides.

4 Preparing the fabric When stiffening fabric yourself, do so before cutting it, as it may shrink slightly. Follow the manufacturer's instructions for the chosen stiffener and allow time for the fabric to dry. The stiffened fabric shouldn't fray so there is no need for hems; if it frays slightly, zigzag the edges with a sewing machine.

5 Measuring up for cutting Measure the length of the roller, excluding the pin ends, and deduct 1cm (⅜in). For the drop, measure from the centre of the brackets to the windowsill, or to just below for a blind hung outside the recess. Add a minimum of 20cm (8in) to allow enough fabric to cover the slat and the roller when the blind is pulled down. Allow extra fabric for pattern matching and centring a design.

3 Cutting the roller to size Measure the distance between the brackets with a steel measuring tape, deduct 3mm (⅛in) to allow for the end cap and saw the roller at the bare end to this length. Fit the cap over the sawn end, then push the pin into the hole and gently hammer it home.

6 Cutting out Lay the fabric out on a flat surface, with any large motif centred. Use a set square and tailor's chalk to mark exact 90° angles at the corners to ensure the fabric is cut on the straight grain so that the blind rolls evenly and hangs well. Using a sharp rotary cutting knife or craft knife and a steel rule as a guide, cut the fabric to size. If widths of fabric need to be joined, overlap the cut edges by 1.5cm (⅝in) and glue with fabric glue.

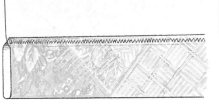

7 Fitting the wooden slat Saw the slat 1cm (⅜in) shorter than the width of the blind. Turn a single 5cm (2in) hem to the wrong side along the bottom edge. Check that the slat slides easily into the casing, and alter if necessary. Machine zigzag stitch close to the edge of the casing. Slide the slat into place, and stitch both ends closed.

8 Attaching cord holder and cord Push one end of the cord through the hole in the cord holder, and knot to secure. Thread the other end of the cord through the acorn and tie a knot. Position the holder in the centre of the casing for the wooden slat, either at the front or back of the blind as preferred, and screw in through the material.

9 Positioning fabric on roller Lay the fabric flat, right side up, and place the roller on top, parallel to the upper edge. Wind the edge of the fabric on to the roller, lining it up with one of the horizontal marks. If your roller has no positioning marks, draw a straight line along the length of the roller at right angles to the edge. Fix the fabric in place temporarily with adhesive tape.

10 Fixing fabric to roller Some kits come with double-sided tape for attaching the blind to the roller. Otherwise, hammer small tacks (or staple) through the edge of the fabric into the roller, spacing evenly 2cm (¾in) apart. Peel off the sticky tape.

TIP
READY STIFFENER
A diluted solution of polyvinyl acetate (PVA) glue can be used to stiffen the fabric. Follow the manufacturer's instructions and use a large container to prevent creasing the fabric too much. If possible work outside – it is a messy procedure.

11 Hanging the blind Roll fabric tightly round the roller by hand and fit into the brackets. Pull blind down to its full extent. Give the cord a gentle tug and the blind should roll up smoothly; if it doesn't, the tension is wrong. Re-roll and repeat until the tension is right.

TRIMMING ROLLER BLINDS

Typically, roller blinds are the simplest of window treatments, made with the neatest outline and fitted with the minimum of trouble. Select any additional decorative details and trimmings to give your blind an original, coordinated look without distracting from this essential simplicity.

You can shape the lower edge of the blind below the wooden slat into an interesting profile by cutting round the outline of the pattern on the fabric or by cutting out geometric shapes, like zigzags and scallops. Alternatively, you can attach a fabric trimming, either in the form of a stiffened panel of fabric to match the curtains or a length of fringing to complement the colours in the blind or in the room.

If you add tabs to the lower edge of the blind, you can thread a curtain rod along the bottom and dispense with the cord pull for raising and lowering it.

▶ *A wide braid or fringing, chosen to complement the blind, is an instant way of finishing the edge. Attach the braid with glue, or stitch or fuse it in place before inserting the wooden slat.*

◀ *Roller blinds provide privacy, so they team well with curtains that are not drawn. The lower edge of these blinds has been finished with a row of tabs which support a brass rod.*

▼ *There are many ways of finishing the lower edge of a roller blind. Here a tuck stitched up from the hem edge holds the batten and a separate tab, made in the same fabric and stitched into the tuck, is used to pull down the blind.*

SHAPED EDGE BLINDS

*For a professional finish on a roller blind, cut the hem
into a distinctive, decorative shape. Add braid, piping or a fringed trim
to emphasize the undulating line of the shaping.*

The method for making a roller blind with a shaped edge is essentially the same as one with a straight edge – stiffened fabric is cut to size and attached to a roller blind fitting. However, with a shaped edge, the batten that straightens and strengthens the hem is positioned higher up, so it is clear of the shaping.. The casing that holds the batten is formed in the upper edge of the shaped hem.

Traditional options for shaping include pretty scallops, elegant Regency-style waved and scooped shapes like a seagull's wing, or lively zigzag points. Alternatively, you can design a shape to suit the mood of the room or the fabric design, by cutting out a deep central point or a castellated edge, or by following the lines of a print motif for the shaping.

A complementary trim that highlights the shaping completes the effect. A neat toning or contrasting bias binding, a pretty picot-edged gimp braid, striped woven tape or a long silky fringe add a final flourish. If the shaped edge follows straight lines you can use any type of braid. For curved shaping, it's better to use a bias binding or a flexible woven braid such as gimp, which bends round the curves without puckering.

The dramatic curves in the shaping of the blinds above contrasts well with the strong stripes of the fabric. The navy braid trim defines the edge and adds a smart finish.

SHAPING A WAVY EDGE

The shaped edge is formed from a double layer of fabric fused together. The stiffened roller blind fabric won't fray, so there is no need to neaten the raw edges. However, you can strengthen them with topstitching, or define the edge with braid or piping. If adding piping, insert it before fusing the layers together. You can topstitch or glue braid in place once the blind is complete.

1 Preparing blind Prepare and cut out the blind, following steps 1-6 on pages 102–103. When cutting fabric length, in addition to the 20cm (13in) required to ensure the roller is hidden when the blind is down, add 25cm (10in) for the shaped section and casing.

2 Making a paper pattern For the width of the pattern, measure the length of the wooden roller, excluding pin ends, and deduct 1cm (⅜in). Decide on the depth of the shaped section, making it about 20cm (8in). On a piece of paper measure and cut out a rectangle of paper to these dimensions.

YOU WILL NEED

- ❖ BLIND FABRIC
- ❖ ROLLER BLIND KIT
- ❖ PATTERN PAPER
- ❖ PENCIL AND RULER
- ❖ PLATE OR FLEXIBLE CURVE (optional)
- ❖ TAILORS' CHALK
- ❖ DOUBLE-SIDED FUSIBLE INTERFACING
- ❖ SEWING THREAD
- ❖ FABRIC ADHESIVE (optional)
- ❖ GIMP OR BRAID TRIM (optional)

▶ *This roller blind is enhanced by the softly waved base shaping, neatly edged in blue gimp braid. It's a perfect choice for a restful bathroom or sparkling white kitchen.*

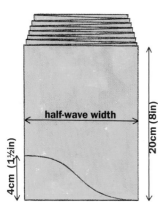

half-wave width

20cm (8in)

4cm (1½in)

3 Drawing shaped pattern To calculate the wave width, divide the blind width by the desired number of wave shapes. Mark the pattern into sections *half* this width and fold concertina-wise at the marks. At first folded edge, mark 4cm (1½in) up from bottom. Using a flexible curve, draw a curved line from the unfolded corner to the mark.

4 Checking pattern With the paper pattern still folded, cut through all the layers then open the pattern out. Check the shaping and adjust it if necessary by refolding and re-cutting it into shape. Or, draw out a new pattern and trim it to the desired shape.

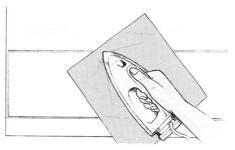

5 Turning up the hem For the casing, measure and mark a line 5cm (2in) up from the lower fabric edge on the wrong side of the fabric. Cut interfacing to the width of the blind by 20cm (8in) deep and position it so it sits above the marked line. Following manufacturer's instructions, fuse interfacing to fabric. Peel off the interfacing paper backing and fold up the hem along top edge of interfacing. Fuse folded layers together.

6 Cutting the shaping Position the paper pattern so the shaped edge sits just up from the lower folded edge. Hold in place with tape or clips as pins may mark the fabric. Using tailors' chalk, mark the shaping lines, and cut along the folded shaped edge.

7 Stitching casing Machine stitch close to the straight raw edge and again 5cm (2in) below to make the casing. For a neat effect on the front of the blind, make stitching as straight as possible. Insert a wooden slat into casing and slipstitch across the short edges. Glue or stitch the trim in place along the shaped edge (optional).

8 Completing the blind Fit the cord holder, fix the fabric to the roller and hang the blind.

TIED BLINDS

Tied blinds are an attractive option for a semi-permanent window dressing. They're quick to make and look smart without appearing too formal. To alter their length, you simply adjust the ties.

A tied blind is basically just a single ungathered curtain, rolled and held in place with ties. It can be lined for added body or left unlined for a more lightweight look. You can hem the lower edge like a normal curtain and let it hang in soft folds at each side of the supporting ties, or you can hold it straight by threading a dowel rod through the hem.

One of the selling points of tied blinds is that they are the easiest style of blind to make. They are also economical on fabric – you need just enough fabric to cover the window area. The unfussy style of the blinds means they work well with curtains too: either make them from the curtain fabric, or from a complementary fabric with the curtain fabric used for the ties. If the blinds are to be used on their own, link them to the rest of the room scheme by using a coordinating fabric for the blind, the ties or both.

Depending on the look you want, you can knot the ties into romantic bows or keep them as simple straps, joined at the base with a press-stud. For a formal effect, use ribbon, braids or plush cords with tassel trims as the ties. For an informal look, team blinds made from serviceable fabrics such as calico with ties in cotton tape or natural cotton cord.

Cream-coloured cotton blinds are linked to the curtains and surrounding scheme by their ties, made from a fabric in the same mellow, autumnal tones as the other soft furnishings.

MAKING A TIED BLIND

The instructions here are for a lined blind with two ribbon ties and an optional, straight lower edge. When choosing lining fabric, make sure the colour matches or is lighter than the main fabric, so that the lining does not cast a dark shadow behind the blind. Use velcro fastening tape to secure the blind to the fixing batten, which is either screwed directly on to the window frame in the recess or to the wall above the window. This quick fixing method is particularly useful for blinds which need to be cleaned frequently.

◄ *For a crisp finish, these ties are interlined and neatly joined at the back of the blind with press-studs. To copy the look, make two ties twice the blind's length, with the short ends unstitched. Attach as below, but so the front half of the ties hangs longer than the back. Hang the blind and roll to the desired length. Wrap the front ties to the back, overlapping the back ties, trim them as necessary and secure with a press-stud.*

1 Measuring up Decide whether to fix the blind in the window recess or above it. Measure the window width to work out the length of batten required. The batten should be the same length as the finished blind, depending on whether it fits neatly into the recess (**A**) or is mounted above and overlaps the frame by 4cm (1½in) on each side (**B**). Screw the batten in place.

2 Cutting out the fabric To calculate the blind length, measure the window from the top of the batten to just below the sill and add on 4cm (1½in) for seam and hem allowances. For the blind width, add 3cm (1¼in) to the batten length. Cut out the main fabric and the lining to these measurements. If joining fabric widths to the required size, match any pattern and press the seams open.

3 Making the blind Pin the main fabric and lining right sides together, with the edges matching. Stitch the sides, taking a 1.5cm (⅝in) seam allowance. Stitch the top and bottom edges, taking a 1cm (⅜in) seam allowance and leaving a gap in the top seam to turn through. Turn the blind right side out and press it. Slipstitch the gap at the top closed, then topstitch close to each side edge to hold the layers together.

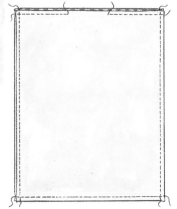

4 Hemming the blind *For a draped hem,* fold 2cm (¾in) to the wrong side and slipstitch it in place, including the side edges. *For a straight hem,* make a casing for the dowel rod – fold 2cm (¾in) to the wrong side and machine stitch this in place, but leave the sides of the hem open.

5 **Making the ribbon ties** Cut two pieces of ribbon 2½ times the length of the blind. Fold each length in half over the top of the blind, placing them about 20cm (8in) in from each side edge, or slightly further in for wide blinds. Stitch across the top of the ties through all layers. Trim the ribbon ends into points.

6 **Attaching the fastenings** Stitch the sewing half of the velcro tape on to the wrong side at the top of the blind. Stick the remaining half of the tape to the front of the batten.

◤ *In a modern setting, the simplicity of a tied blind is appealing. Stiffening the lower edge of the blind with a length of dowel ensures that it hangs level across a window while the stripes emphasize its height.*

7 **Hanging the blind** If required, insert the dowel rod in the channel hem and stitch the side edges closed to encase it. To hang the blind, press the two parts of the fastening tape together. Roll up the blind to the required height and hold it temporarily in place at each side with clothes pegs. Tie the ribbons into bows.

TIP

JOINING FABRIC WIDTHS

As tied blinds are made from ungathered fabric, it is often possible to make a blind from a single fabric width. If joins are necessary to accommodate the window width, plan to cut the fabric with a central panel, and position the joining seams each side of this so that the seams are hidden behind the ties. The lining fabric should be cut and joined to match in the same way.

Tied blinds can have many different looks, depending on the fabrics used, the way the blinds are rolled, with or without a dowel rod, and what the ties are made from.

▶ *This inexpensive calico blind is given a smart touch and linked to surrounding paintwork by a narrow navy border down each side edge. The casual fashion in which it's tied up with cotton tape strikes just the right note for the informal conservatory setting.*

◢ *Four narrow tied blinds, made in a natural cotton with a stiffened lower edge, make an eye-catching, distinctive window treatment. Rolling them to different heights adds to their charm.*

▲ *An open cupboard is given a lively new look when it is painted Wedgwood blue and fitted with a jolly tied blind. When lowered, the blind conceals the contents of the cupboard; raised as shown, it is appreciated on its purely decorative merit.*

RUCHED BLINDS

The ruched swags and folds of Austrian and festoon blinds soften any window shape, and create a style that strikes a balance between curtains and the simple lines of other blinds.

Ruched blinds are a truly versatile style of window dressing. Their soft lines can create dramatically different looks that range from the unashamedly romantic, in floral chintz or frilly lace, to sophisticated silk swags, or low-key styles using inexpensive cotton fabric and muslin. The blinds can be lined or unlined, and are best made from lightweight fabrics and sheers. Use them on their own or to complement matching drapes; in a sheer fabric they make a charming alternative to net curtains.

A ruched blind is basically a single curtain that's gathered across the top with curtain heading tape. A series of cords spaced vertically up the back of the blind are pulled to raise or lower it. The difference between Austrian and festoon blinds is most noticeable when the blinds are lowered. On Austrian blinds the fullness of the ruched swags depends on the blind's position – when lowered the swags drop to hem level, leaving a softly gathered curtain effect above. A festoon blind is permanently ruched into flounces all the way down its length with gathering tape, whether raised or lowered.

You can trim either style of blind with frills and piping, and gather the tops with different styles of heading tape – from informal standard tape to neat pencil pleat or triple pleat tape.

An Austrian blind in a soft muted print creates a look that's well dressed without being overly fussy.

MAKING RUCHED BLINDS

There are various ways to make and operate ruched blinds, and a choice of fixing options. To pull up the blind, you can use special looped and corded tape, or thread cords through rings stitched at regular intervals up the back of the blind. To hang the blind, you can use a special ruched blind track, or a standard curtain track fixed to a wooden batten.

The play of light and shade on the ruched, swagged fabric is a feature of these blinds, so shiny fabrics such as chintz and moiré or translucent sheers are a good choice. The best effects are uncluttered, so plains, softly coloured patterns, vertical stripes and small prints work well. Avoid using fabrics with dominant or isolated pattern motifs as these may not show to advantage.

On wide windows it is best to hang two blinds side by side, as the weight of the fabric could cause a very large blind to sag.

◾ *A goblet-pleat heading shows to advantage the distinctive teacup print on this Austrian blind.*

MAKING AN AUSTRIAN BLIND

These instructions are for a lined blind with a folded frill edge. The cords that operate the blind are threaded through looped Austrian blind tape and the blind is mounted on a special ruched blind track, available in kit form from drapery stores. If you prefer, you can hang the blind from a standard curtain track; see *Making a Festoon Blind* (page 115) for this method.

MEASURING UP FOR THE BLIND

1 Fitting the track Fix the blind track in place over the window, either to the top of the window recess, or outside the window recess, and extended by 5-10cm (2-4in) on each side so the blind blocks out the light effectively.

2 Calculating the width To find the blind width, multiply the track length by 2½ – this will give you a generously gathered blind using pencil pleat heading tape. Divide this figure by the width of your fabric to determine how many fabric widths are required to make up the Austrian blind, rounding up the measurement if necessary.

3 Calculating the drop To find the blind drop, measure from the track down to the sill and add 45cm (18in) for turnings and to ensure the bottom of the blind remains swagged when it is fully lowered. To calculate the total amount of fabric needed for the basic blind and lining, multiply the blind drop by the number of fabric widths required, adding on a little extra for pattern matching if necessary. Also allow extra fabric for the frill (see *Cutting out the Blind*, step 2, opposite).

4 Measuring for swags Decide how many swags you would like the blind to have: the vertical Austrian blind tapes used to create the swags are usually placed about 60-75cm (23-30in) apart, to give swags of 24-30cm (9-12in) on the finished blind, once it has been gathered across its width. Choose a swag size which divides evenly into the width of the ungathered blind.

Measuring for tape and cord To estimate for the length of blind tape required (red in diagram), allow for tape to run down each side of each swag, including the blind's side edges. Allow a little extra on each length for turnings. To estimate for the cord required (blue in diagram) for each tape, each cord should be 1½ times the tape length, plus the distance from the top of the tape to the corner of the blind on what will be the fastening cleat side.

◣ The simple lines of plain white Austrian blinds are all that's needed to dress these handsome windows. Raised to a flattering height, the soft folds of the blinds act as a visual foil for the long, straight lines of the windows and elegant wall panelling.

CUTTING OUT THE BLIND

Joining the fabric widths Cut out the main fabric to the correct size, adding a 1.5cm (⅝in) seam allowance all round; join fabric widths where necessary, matching patterns across the seams. Cut out the lining to the same size, but deduct 2cm (¾in) from the length. Join the fabric widths and press the seams open.

Preparing the frill strip For a double-sided frill, cut out and join widths of the main fabric, cutting along the straight grain and matching patterns if necessary, to make up a strip 17cm (6¾in) deep, and twice the length of the blind, plus its width, multiplied by 1½-2. Press the seams open. Fold the strip in half lengthways with wrong sides together and press to make a folded frill.

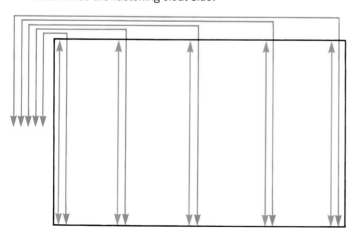

MAKING UP THE BLIND

1 Adding the frill Run two lines of gathering stitches, 6mm (¼in) and 1.5cm (⅝in) in from the raw frill edges. Draw up the frill to fit round the two sides and lower edge of the blind. Lay out the main fabric, right side up. Pin, tack and stitch the frill in place to the right side of the main fabric, with the raw edges level.

2 Attaching the lining Lay the main fabric flat with the lining on top, right sides together with side and lower edges matching. Taking 1.5cm (⅝in) seams, pin then stitch through all layers, down the sides and across the lower edge. Snip across corners and turn right side out. Press flat, and tack across top edge.

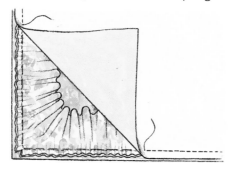

3 Stitching on the looped tapes Lay the blind flat with the lining up. Chalk the positions of the tapes on the lining. Cut each length of blind tape to the length of the lining plus 1cm (⅜in). When cutting the tape, make sure that the bottom loop on each length lies 6cm (2⅜in) from the end of the tape, so that the blind will pull up evenly. Turn 1cm (⅜in) to the wrong side at the bottom of each tape, then pin, tack and stitch the tapes in position through all the fabric layers.

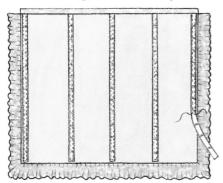

4 Attaching the heading tape Cut a length of pencil-pleat heading tape the width of the blind, plus a little extra for neatening. At the top of the blind, fold the overlapping 2cm (¾in) of main fabric over the lining to enclose its raw edge. Place the pencil-pleat heading tape on top of this turned edge, covering the raw edges of the fabric and vertical tapes. Stitch the heading tape in place. Draw up the heading tape to fit the window.

▲ A generous centre swag is an attractive variation for an Austrian blind, especially when simple lines are preferred.

TIP
CORDS AND RINGS
The outlines of Austrian blind tape can sometimes show through a lightweight fabric. To avoid this, stitch transparent curtain rings at intervals down the back of the blind instead, and thread non-stretch cords through the rings.

5 Threading the cords For each vertical tape, cut a length of cord long enough to run up the tape, across the top of the blind and halfway down the side. On each tape, knot the cord to the bottom loop and thread it up through the loops to the top of the tape.

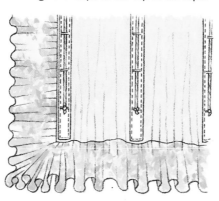

6 Mounting the blind Remove the track from its wall brackets and hook the blind on to the track. Adjust the position of the track eyelets (**a**) so that there is one above each vertical blind tape. Thread the cords through the eyelet above, then through all the other eyelets along the track, until all the cords are at one side of the blind. Replace the blind track on its brackets. Fix the cleat to the wall or window frame next to the blind, within easy reach.

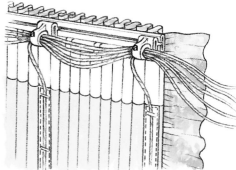

7 Adjusting the blind Pull the cords to check that the blind can be raised and lowered evenly, and adjust them where necessary. Once satisfied, lower the blind to the sill and check that all the cords are straight, before knotting them at the end of the track. Plait the cords together to make a simple pulley cord or use a special cord tidy. Trim the ends with scissors to neaten, and fit a pull. Secure the cords around the cleat.

MAKING A FESTOON BLIND

A festoon blind is made in almost the same way as an Austrian blind, but the vertical tapes are threaded with gathering cords to pull the blind up into permanent ruches. For the vertical tapes, you can either use special festoon blind tape or improvise with standard curtain heading tape and split curtain rings. Because of the ruches, the blind takes much more fabric than an Austrian blind – for each fabric width needed, you require 1½-3 times the required finished blind length; as a guide, for a lined blind allow at least 1½ times the finished length, and for unlined or sheer fabrics allow 2-3 times this length for a luxurious effect.

The instructions given overleaf are for a lined blind. If you want to make an unlined blind, omit the frill and simply neaten the fabric edges with narrow double hems. The steps show how to fix the blind to a standard curtain track mounted on to a wooden batten. The cords on the blind pass through metal eyelets which are screwed to the batten, under the track. If you prefer, you can mount the blind on a ruched blind track, as in *Making an Austrian Blind*.

▼ *This lined, piped and frill-trimmed festoon blind softens the window shape, adding a warm touch to what could otherwise be a blank corner.*

YOU WILL NEED

❖ WOODEN BATTEN
❖ CURTAIN TRACK
❖ MAIN FABRIC
❖ LINING FABRIC
❖ PREPARED PIPING CORD (optional)
❖ CORDED FESTOON BLIND TAPE OR LIGHTWEIGHT STANDARD CURTAIN TAPE AND SMALL SPLIT CURTAIN RINGS
❖ NON-STRETCH CORD
❖ PENCIL PLEAT HEADING TAPE
❖ SCREW EYES
❖ CURTAIN HOOKS
❖ FESTOON WEIGHTS (optional)

1 Measuring up Fit the batten in place, and fit the track to it. To estimate the main fabric and lining requirements, calculate the blind width and drop as for *Making an Austrian Blind, Measuring up for the Blind*, steps 2-3, but allow up to three times the finished blind length for each fabric width, as required; allow extra fabric for the frill. Measure and estimate for swags and tape and cord amounts as for *Making an Austrian Blind, Measuring up for the Blind*, steps 4-5. Multiply the unruched blind drop by two and add the width to find how much covered piping you need, if desired.

☑ *The permanently ruched gathers on a festoon blind are shown to advantage with translucent sheers, as light can filter through even when the blind is lowered.*

2 Making the blind Prepare the blind and frill as for *Making an Austrian Blind, Cutting out the Blind*. Make up the blind as for *Making an Austrian Blind, Making up the Blind*, steps 1-4, adding the the piping, if desired, before the frill, and substituting corded festoon blind tape or lightweight standard tape for the vertical Austrian blind tapes. Attach the heading tape, but do not pull up the threads yet.

3 Gathering the tapes If using standard curtain tape (as shown here), slip split rings into the pockets in the vertical tapes at regular intervals, making sure they lie evenly across the blind's width. Draw up the vertical tapes to give the appropriate drop to the blind, and draw up the curtain heading tape to match the length of the track.

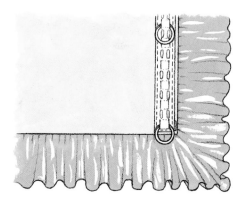

4 Adding the cords Cut lengths of cord as for *Making an Austrian Blind, Making up the Blind*, step 5, and knot each cord to the bottom ring on each vertical tape. Thread the cords through the rings to the top of the tapes.

5 Hanging the blind Fit a row of screw eyes to the lower edge of the batten, so each eye coincides with a vertical tape on the blind. Insert curtain hooks in the heading tape and hang the blind in place. Thread the cords through the screw eyes and bring them to one side of the blind. Knot them and secure them to a cleat. For sheer or lightweight fabrics, stitch a festoon weight to the lower edge of the blind, at each side, to help the blind move up and down smoothly.

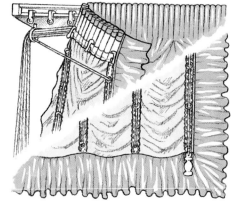

CHOOSING NON-FABRIC BLINDS

*Non-fabric blinds are a more streamlined window treatment
than curtains and frilled or pleated fabric blinds. They also cut out
glare from bright sunlight and provide privacy.*

Non-fabric blinds combine all the practical benefits of their fabric counterparts with a crisper, cleaner finish. Like fabric blinds, they allow you to adjust the amount of light entering the room quickly and easily and provide a screen against an ugly view or prying eyes. Non-fabric blinds also have the advantages of drawing right back from the window, forming a neat, unobtrusive strip at the top or sides and allowing a maximum of light to flood in – a real bonus for tiny windows and ones with a shady outlook.

There is a huge range of non-fabric blinds to choose from and you'll find styles to suit all budgets and decorative schemes. Most smaller non-fabric blinds are operated manually with cords or rods to open or close them. Some heavier blinds are operated with belts or winch handles. You can also set up any type of non-fabric blind to operate by remote control.

You can buy made-to-measure non-fabric blinds and a wide range of standard sizes from many large stores. Most department stores stock a large variety of styles which come with instructions on cutting to fit.

Sleek wooden Venetian blinds are a chic and practical choice of window treatment for this modern interior. The wooden slats echo the natural materials and warm tones used throughout the scheme.

STYLE CHECKLIST

There are many different styles of non-fabric blinds in a variety of materials. The main types are listed below.

PLEATED BLINDS

Traditionally, pleated blinds were made of strengthened sun- and water-resistant paper. Nowadays you can also get them in polyester. The blinds have permanent accordion-style horizontal pleats with cords to draw them up. They cut out glare, but most do not provide night-time privacy. They do have excellent insulating properties, however, keeping the interior warm in winter and cool in summer. The newest pleated blinds have a honeycomb sructure which helps the pleats keep their shape across wide windows and traps air in the cells for extra insulation. Pleated blinds usually come with 2.5cm (1in) pleats, in a range of plain colours and flecked finishes.

ROLL-UP BLINDS

There are all sorts of non-fabric roll-up blinds – woven grass, bamboo, split cane or pinoleum (wooden reed) and PVC. Horizontal strips of material are stitched together to hold them in position, and bound at the edges. The blinds are rolled up via a pulley system. Finishes include plain white or colours for PVC, while the other materials look good in their natural state, colour-stained or with a painted design.

VENETIAN BLINDS

Venetian blinds are the most versatile of non-fabric blinds. You can close them to shut out light and give total privacy, angle them for soft shading or raise them above the window to leave a clear view. The principle is simple. With the blind lowered, you twist the slats to the angle which gives the right amount of light – usually by pulling a cord. With the slats in the horizontal (full open) position, pulling on a second cord stacks the slats and raises them out of the way of the window.

Venetian blinds come in natural or stained timber, plastic and aluminium. They are available in a huge range of colours and patterns. You can also get blinds with perforated slats to provide a gentle diffusion of light when closed.

VERTICAL LOUVRE BLINDS

These blinds are like Venetian blinds turned on their sides, with louvres (vanes) which rotate on a vertical axis to let in or shut out light. Like Venetian blinds, the angle of the louvres is adjusted by a cord at the side of the window, while a separate cord pulls the louvres right back to one or both sides. Vertical blinds come in a wide choice of colours and materials, from laminated PVC or fibreglass to aluminium.

SHUTTERS

Shutters perform a similar function to blinds. For centuries they have kept out summer sunshine in hot countries, and helped to combat cold and winds in cooler climes, while providing privacy and security.

Internal shutters, so popular in Georgian times, are still widely available today in traditional panelled designs in natural softwoods that can be clear-varnished, stained or painted. Colonial-style slatted wood plantation shutters are the alternative. You can adjust the angle of plantation shutter slats by moving a central bar, allowing more or less light into the room. With panelled shutters this is clearly not an option.

Roll-down shutters that are operated from inside by a cranking handle are designed primarily for security, but they also provide good insulation. You can fit them internally or externally. Made to measure, they come in a wide range of attractive colours.

Clever paperwork

Semi-opaque, roll-up paper blinds fixed across a wide expanse of window provide daytime privacy and shade, without blocking out the light completely.

Filtered rays

The angled slats of a wooden Venetian blind filter just enough of the sun's strong rays to allow the owner of this rocking chair to read in comfort.

Tall and slender

The long, slim shape of this Venetian blind and the rich colouring of its red-stained wooden slats match the elegant lines and timber of the dining room furniture. The blind creates the illusion of a much larger window and is ideal for concealing an ugly view without blocking out all the natural light.

Keeping the heat in

This pleated 'honeycomb' blind has a special layer which traps heat, making it a good choice for rooms in which insulation is important.

Sun trap

A neat, plastic Venetian blind in cool ice-blue is the perfect choice for a large window that faces the sun. Angled slats filter the harsh sunlight, casting an attractive shadow on the wall.

Concertina pleats

Pleated paper blinds have a streamlined appearance that's perfectly suited to a modern kitchen. Here, smokey grey pleated blinds pick up the tones of a slate-coloured work surface, a stainless steel sink and chrome tap.

WHERE TO USE NON-FABRIC BLINDS

You can fit non-fabric blinds in any room, but some types are more suited to certain situations.

LIVING ROOMS AND BEDROOMS

In rooms used for relaxation or sleep you need a window treatment that cuts out the light and, in most cases, provides privacy. Vertical louvre and Venetian blinds are a good choice for large picture windows, as you can leave the blind in position while twisting the louvres to let in or block out light.

To soften the hard outline of a non-fabric blind, you can add floor-length curtains, or a valance or pelmet which will hide a horizontally pleated blind completely when it is drawn up.

▶*Winning team*
Combining a delicate rattan cane blind with a pretty pair of floral curtains is as practical as it's pretty – the lowered blind gives a restful, dappled light during the day, while the curtains act as a total blackout at night.

◢ *Panelled elegance*
Painted white or stripped and varnished, Georgian-style panelled shutters give an impression of height to a room and add period elegance.

KITCHENS

Non-fabric blinds are ideal for kitchen windows. They are easy to clean and don't absorb food smells. The sleek lines of plastic or aluminium Venetian blinds reinforce the theme of a modern kitchen, while natural timber slats or roll-up cane blinds blend beautifully with a country kitchen.

BATHROOMS AND CLOAKROOMS

Here Venetian blinds are once again an ideal choice, as they provide complete privacy and some insulation when closed. You can partially open the slats during the day to allow light into the room without losing privacy altogether. Non-fabric blinds don't suffer from condensation; you can just wipe them down – a great bonus in a bathroom.

CONSERVATORIES

Fitting adjustable blinds in a conservatory alleviates the problem of heat build-up. When the sun is at its hottest you can close the blinds to lessen the chance of indoor plants wilting or being scorched. At other times you just have to pull them up to let the light come flooding in. In a conservatory crowded with plants, blinds are less likely than curtains to get entangled in foliage.

Conservatory roof blinds are even more effective at counteracting the consequences of strong sunlight. You can order made-to-measure roof blinds or buy blinds designed to be cut to fit the shape of your conservatory roof at home.

◁ *The effective fold-up*
This Roman-type pinoleum (wooden reed) blind in sunny yellow is a cost-effective way to treat a window. You can stain or paint a blind like this to match the decor perfectly.

▽ *Airy option*
White-painted plantation shutters evoke the airy splendour of colonial homes of old. They're an ideal choice for a bedroom, teaming privacy with a light, fresh and open feel.

◢ *Now you see them, then you don't*
With a single twist, these vertical louvre blinds can swing open to reveal the garden.

MEASURING UP

You must measure and fit your blinds correctly to get the best out of them. If you decide to fit the blind inside a window recess, measure the recess width and the drop from the top of the recess to the bottom. If you hang the blind outside the recess you can make it whatever width and drop you like, creating the illusion of a larger window area. Whatever your requirements, an overlap of no less than 7.5cm (3in) is best. On a large picture window you may choose to take the blind from ceiling to floor, covering the whole wall as well as the window.

Wherever you are fitting a blind, use a steel rule to measure in two or three places both horizontally and vertically in case the window is slightly irregular. Double-check the measurements before ordering a made-to-measure blind.

Buy a blind in the next size up if you intend to cut it to size yourself. Most blinds that you can cut to fit come with instructions. Blind cutters for cutting metal slats are available.

▶ Security matters

Security shutters can do more than just protect. This green external shutter gives the outside of the house a smart finish and blends with the climbing foliage.

◢ Shady solutions

Here, roll-up pinoleum side blinds are sprayed to match the rest of the conservatory, while man-made fabric roof blinds made from fibreglass screen out the sun and excess heat without obscuring vision.

◣ Perfect for privacy

You can pull the bottom half of these 'top down blinds' up to the middle of the window for privacy, pull the top down for shade or pull both halves together for a complete blackout.

PAINTING A VENETIAN BLIND

Inexpensive white Venetian blinds take on a bold new look with a lick of paint. Choose colours to tie in with your room scheme and treat your windows to a new, streamlined image.

Customize a blind to work with your existing scheme. Here a simple sponged effect links the blind to the rest of the room.

Venetian blinds are a practical window covering – the slats can be angled to allow maximum light through, or lowered to diffuse a soft light into the room. Used on their own they have a sleek modern look, yet teamed with curtains they fit into a more traditional scheme.

Combine the practicality of Venetian blinds with one of the following paint effect ideas for an inexpensive window treatment to fit in exactly with your existing room scheme. You can paint the blinds in any bright colour, or for a jazzy striped effect, try painting the individual slats in different colours. Alternatively, try a simple all-over paint effect like sponging or you can even stencil or paint designs free-hand on the blind.

Look for a PVC blind – cheaper and easier to paint than a metal one. It should have a matt surface which takes paint well. Any solvent based paint is suitable – car spray paints work particularly well. Emulsion/latex paints do adhere to the surface of the blind, but they need to be fixed with a spray varnish for a durable finish.

Painting a Striped Blind

Car spray paints give a smooth, slightly shiny finish to the blinds which suits a striped effect. If you decide to use spray paint, try to work outdoors as the fumes are strong and the spray messy. If you have to do it indoors, make sure there is adequate ventilation and protect the surrounding areas with newspaper.

To avoid getting paint on the cords, it is best to unthread and remove the slats. Before undoing the blind, work out the pattern – do you want a single band of colour along the lower edge, or narrow or wide stripes down the entire blind?

To remove the slats, follow the manufacturer's instructions for shortening the blind. Once the cords are unplugged from the base, it is easy to slide each slat out, and replace them later.

YOU WILL NEED

❖ READY-MADE BLIND
❖ NEWSPAPER
❖ RUBBER GLOVES
❖ CAR SPRAY PAINT in colours of your choice

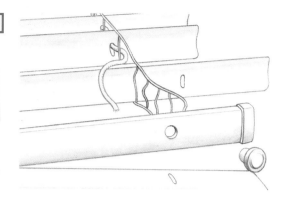

1 Planning your design Decide roughly how wide you want the stripes to be – for example, one, two or three slats wide. Then count the total number of slats and work out how many you have to paint in each colour, and how many you should leave unpainted for the full effect.

2 Preparing to paint Follow the manufacturer's instructions to release the cords and remove the individual slats. Spread newspaper on the floor or other large flat surface and lay out the number of slats you want to paint in the first colour. Make sure the area is well ventilated.

3 Painting the slats Wearing rubber gloves and following the paint manufacturer's instructions, spray colour on to the slats. Use a steady, sweeping motion to ensure even coverage. Allow the paint to dry, then turn the slats over and paint the other side in the same way.

4 Painting further colours Repeat step 3, painting the remaining slats in your chosen colours. Allow them to dry overnight before re-threading them in the right order on to the cords of the blind.

◀ *Two shades of blue, with some slats left white, is just the right look for this pleasing bathroom blind.*

▶ *For a quick and attractive result, keep half of the slats white and paint the rest in one solid colour – as with this dramatic black and white blind.*

USING A PAINT EFFECT

YOU WILL NEED

- ❖ EGGSHELL/FLAT SATIN PAINT in two shades of the same colour
- ❖ PAINT BRUSH 12mm (½in)
- ❖ ARTIST'S PAINT BRUSH
- ❖ NEWSPAPER
- ❖ SPONGE
- ❖ OLD SAUCER
- ❖ WHITE/MINERAL SPIRIT
- ❖ GOLD WAX (optional)

A paint effect is more subtle than the graphic look of stripes. Sponging works particularly well on blinds – work it in two similar coloured paints to get a soft-textured finish. This blind has two shades of aqua eggshell/flat satin, with touches of gold to add depth.

You can paint the blind without taking the slats apart – though you must take care to avoid getting paint on the cords. Use a fine artist's paint brush to apply paint around that area. To make it easier to paint the base colour suspend the blind in a doorway or tie it up at an accessible window and hold the end of each slat as you paint it. Lay the blind flat on a firm surface for sponging.

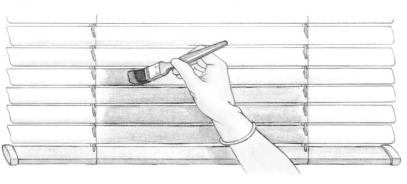

1 Painting the base colour Hang the blind in a place where you can work on it comfortably. Apply the base colour to the topside of the slats, using the paint brush for the main area and the artist's brush to get in around the holes for the cords. Allow the slats to dry, then turn the blind around and paint the undersides in the same way. Leave the paint to dry overnight.

2 Sponging on a second colour Protect the work surface with newspaper and lay the blind flat on top. Tip a little of the second colour into a saucer. Dip the sponge in the paint and lightly dab it all over the front of the blind. Allow it to dry overnight. You don't need to sponge the underside.

3 Adding gold highlights (optional) Using a new or clean piece of sponge, dab gold wax (or paint) sparingly over the front of the blind. Allow it to dry completely before you hang the blind up.

◢ *Make your sponged blind shimmer by dabbing on a small amount of gold wax. Here, the gold echoes the stars on the wallpaper and makes a pleasing background for a golden candlestick.*

Index

ACKNOWLEDGEMENTS

Photographs

7 IPC Magazines/Robert Harding Syndication, 8(t) Romo, 8(bl) EWA/Brian Harrison, 8(br) Paul Ryan, 9, 10(t) IPC Magazines/Robert Harding Syndication, 10(b) Harlequin, 11(t) EWA/Michael Dunne, 11(b) EWA/Andreas von Einsiedel, 12(tl) Eaglemoss/Simon Page-Ritchie, 12(tr) Romo, 12(cl) Marie Claire Maison/Tosi, 12(cr) Marie Claire Maison/Comte, 12(bl) Kestrel, 12(br) IPC Magazines/Robert Harding Syndication, 17 Ametex, 19 Eaglemoss/Tif Hunter, 21 Eaglemoss/John Suett, 23(bl) Rufflette, 23(br), 24(tl,cl,br) Eaglemoss/Graham Rae, 24(tr,cr,bl,bc) Eaglemoss/Tif Hunter, 24(c) Rufflette, 25 Integra Products, 26 IPC Magazines/Robert Harding Syndication, 27 EWA/Spike Powell, 28-29 IPC Magazines/Robert Harding Syndication, 29(br), 30 Eaglemoss/Paul Bricknell, 31 Ariadne Holland, 32, 33 Eaglemoss/Graham Rae, 34(tr) EWA/Michael Dunne, 34(bl) IPC Magazines/Robert Harding Syndication, 34(br) EWA/Neil Lorimer, 35 IPC Magazines/Robert Harding Syndication, 36-37 EWA/Nadia McKenzie, 38 IPC Magazines/Robert Harding Syndication, 39 Laura Ashley, 40 Anna French, 41 IPC Magazines/Robert Harding Syndication, 42(t) EWA/Shona Wood, 42(bl) Textra, 42(br) Marie Claire IdÇes/Chauvin/Chastres/Lancrenon, 43

Christian Fischbacher, 44, 45 Eaglemoss/Martin Chaffer, 46 Romo, 47 Sanderson, 48 IPC Magazines/Robert Harding Syndication, 49 Harrison Drape, 50-51(tl) Harlequin, 51(tr) Home Flair, 52 Marvic Textiles, 53, 55, 56 Stiebel of Nottingham, 57 Eaglemoss/Steve Tanner, 58 Stiebel of Nottingham, 59 IPC Magazines/Robert Harding Syndication, 60-61 Eaglemoss/Steve Tanner, 62(t) IPC Magazines/Robert Harding Syndication, 62(b) Eaglemoss/Steve Tanner, 65 Paul Ryan, 67 IPC Magazines/Robert Harding Syndication, 68 Eaglemoss/Steve Tanner, 69 Jane Churchill, 70 Sanderson, 71 IPC Magazines/Robert Harding Syndication, 72 EWA/Michael Dunne, 74 EWA/Andreas von Einsiedel, 75 Butterick/Vogue, 76(t) EWA/Andreas von Einsiedel, 76(bl) EWA/Peter Woloszynski, 76(br) Laura Ashley, 77 Habitat, 78 Jali,79 Eaglemoss/Simon Page-Ritchie, 80(t,br) IPC Magazines/Robert Harding Syndication, 80(bl) Ariadne Holland, 81, 82(cl) Eaglemoss/Iain Bagwell, 82(tl) IPC Magazines/Robert Harding Syndication, 82-83(bl) Sanderson, 84 Rufflette, 85-86, 87 Eaglemoss/Simon Page-Ritchie, 88, 89 Eaglemoss/Graham Rae, 90 Eaglemoss/Simon Page-Ritchie, 91 Abode, 92 Ariadne Holland, 93, 94, 95(t,br) Eaglemoss/Steve Tanner, 95(bl) IPC Magazines/Robert Harding Syndication, 96 Eaglemoss/Paul Bricknell, 97(t) IPC Magazines/Robert Harding Syndication, 97(br) Eaglemoss/Mark Wood, 98(tl) IPC Magazines/Robert Harding Syndication, 98(tr,cl) Tempus

Stet, 98(bl) Harrison Drape, 98(cr,br) Eaglemoss/Graham Rae, 101 Marie Claire IdÇes/Hussenot/Chastres/Lancrenon, 102 Shand Kydd, 104(t) Romo, 104(bl) EWA/Brian Harrison, 104(br) EWA/Rodney Hyett, 105, 106 IPC Magazines/Robert Harding Syndication, 107 Colefax & Fowler, 108 Ariadne Holland, 109 Laura Ashley, 110(t,br) IPC Magazines/Robert Harding Syndication, 110(bl) Ariadne Holland, 111 Crowson Fabrics, 112 IPC Magazines/Robert Harding Syndication, 113 EWA/Neil Lorimer, 114 EWA/Simon Upton, 115 Abode, 116 EWA/Rodney Hyett, 117 IPC Magazines/Robert Harding Syndication, 118(t) EWA/Rodney Hyett, 118(b) Ikea, 119(tl) Sunway Blinds, 119(tr) Luxaflex Blinds, 119(c) EWA/Debi Treloar 119(b) EWA/Rodney Hyett, 120(t) EWA/Debi Treloar, 120(b) EWA/Andreas von Einsiedel, 121(t) Sunway Blinds, 121(bl) EWA/Rodney Hyett, 121(br) EWA/Neil Lorimer, 122(t) Filtrasol, 122(bl) Appeal Blinds, 122(br) Luxaflex, 123-126 Eaglemoss/Graham Rae.

Illustrations

13-16, 19-22 Terry Evans, 28-30, 32, 36-38, 44-45, 48, 50-52, 54, 57-58, 60-63 John Hutchinson, 64 Terry Evans, 66-68, 70, 72-75 John Hutchinson, 78-79 Coral Mula, 82-84 John Hutchinson, 88-90 Sally Holmes, 92, 94-96, 102-103, 106, 108-109, 113-116 John Hutchinson, 124, 126 Coral Mula.